SERVING WITH LOVE

Simple, time-saving ideas for entertainment for anything from birthday parties to after-church snacks . . . ways to take special thought of your family and neighbors . . . reflections of life, love and your home . . . "recipes" for discontent and for devotion . . .

. . . all make FOOD AND FELLOWSHIP IN THE CHRISTIAN HOME a "living" book as well as a unique cookbook of the memorable desserts, treats and main dishes that will delight your family.

Food and Fellowship
in the Christian Home

ELIZABETH S. PISTOLE

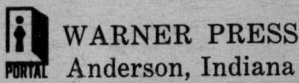 WARNER PRESS
Anderson, Indiana

FOOD AND FELLOWSHIP

A PORTAL Book
Published by Keats Publishing, Inc. for
Warner Press, Inc.

PORTAL Books edition published January, 1973

Copyright © 1965 by Warner Press, Inc.

All Rights Reserved
Library of Congress Catalog Number: 65-12587
ISBN: 0 87162 148 7

Printed in the United States of America

PORTAL Books are published by Warner Press, Inc.
1200 East 5th Street,
Anderson, Indiana 46011

Contents

IT'S TIME ...   Page

To Introduce	7
To Appreciate	8
To Measure Up	9
To Review Terms	10
To Plan	13
To Watch the Calories	13
To Be Nosy	14
To Be Special	15
To Talk	17
To Entertain	18
To Take Inventory	21
To Keep Christmas	21
To Remember	22
To Dig	24
To Perk Up	24
To Hobo	26
To See Through Children's Eyes	27
To Color	28
To Stew	28
To Portray	30
To Season	31
To Devote	32

FOR RECIPES

Beverages	33
Breads	36
Cakes	45
Candy	59
Cookies	62

	Page
Desserts	77
Meat Dishes	85
This 'n' That	99
Pastries and Pies	104
Salads	114
Seafoods	121
Vegetables	124

IT'S TIME . . .

To Introduce

It's time to turn off the burner, pour a cup of coffee, and relax while we lift the lid off this book. It has recipes for tasty foods and zesty living. It has a recipe for a perfect strawberry glacé pie as well as one for cooking a husband. It suggests fun times, special activity times, and quiet simmering times.

Your popularity as a cook begins right there in your own kitchen—
> when you plan carefully,
>> buy wisely,
>>> prepare skillfully,
>>>> and serve appetizing,
>>>>> attractive meals.

And you have so many roles to fill! You are chef for the family; you host committee and club meetings; you hold your breath while Susie experiments and learns to cook; you entertain relatives for the traditional Thanksgiving dinner; and you stand discreetly aside while teen-agers invade the kitchen to whip up a pizza.

So it's time you took a moment to appreciate yourself and to pay yourself a delectable compliment. Stand up and give three cheers for the queen of the kitchen—YOU!

IT'S TIME . . .

To Appreciate

Recipes used in this book come from a wide variety of friends, relatives, club members, and family experiments. A special word of thanks must be given to my family for their endurance while I "stewed" over this book. I have a suspicion that there will be a celebration when I get back to my "home on the range." The children: Cindy, Carole, David, and John have resisted the urge to go on a hunger strike when they found the kitchen table cluttered with recipes instead of food. My husband, Hollis, has survived my cooking experiments and is my official taster of new recipes and unusual creations attempted in the kitchen. He is the best potato masher-upper in the country! But most of all I appreciate the pleased look as he samples a spoonful of some strange, new concoction that I have made.

So now you know my secret—I married a guinea pig!

IT'S TIME . . .
To Measure Up

Good cooks always measure carefully. Our modern recipes call for level measurements and standard measuring cups and spoons. Good cooks know that substitutions do change a recipe. You may end up with a substitute menu. Proper measurements, right size pans, correct oven temperatures, and sticking to the recipe will stabilize your efforts. In case you ever need a reminder, some of the measurements are:

- 3 teaspoons=1 tablespoon
- 4 tablespoons=¼ cup
- 8 tablespoons=½ cup
- 16 tablespoons=1 cup
- 1 cup=8 ounces
- 2 cups=1 pint
- 4 cups=1 quart
- 4 quarts=1 gallon
- 2 tablespoons butter=1 ounce
- ½ cup butter=1 stick
- 2¼ cups packed brown sugar=1 pound
- 3½ cups sifted confectioners' sugar=1 pound
- 4 cups sifted flour=1 pound
- 1 cup chopped nuts=¼ pound
- 15 marshmallows=¼ pound
- 6½ tablespoons cream cheese=one 3-ounce package
- 11 crumbled graham crackers=1 cup
- 1½ tablespoons vinegar or 1½ tablespoons lemon juice added to sweet milk to make 1 cup of sour milk
- 12 to 14 egg yolks=1 cup
- 8 to 10 egg whites=1 cup
- 4 cups grated American cheese=1 pound
- 1 lemon=3 to 4 tablespoons juice

HOW MUCH IS IN A CAN?
(found on label of can)

- No. 300 = 1¾ cup
- No. 303 = 2 cups
- No. 2 = 2½ cups
- No. 3 = 4 cups
- No. 10 = 12 to 13 cups

IT'S TIME . . .

To Review Terms

A

Au gratin—A browned covering of bread crumbs usually mixed with butter or cheese.

B

Bake—Cook in the oven.

Barbecue—Roast meat on a grill over hot coals, periodically basting it with a sauce.

Baste—Spoon liquid or fat over food while it is cooking.

Beat—Mix fast with spoon or beater to make smooth.

Blanch—Plunge into boiling water, then into cold water.

Blend—Mix ingredients until smooth.

Boil—Cook in liquid so hot that bubbles break on the surface.

Bouillon—A clear meat broth.

Broil—Cook directly under heating unit.

C

Canapé—Small piece of fried or toasted bread topped with sea food, cheese, or meat.

Caramelize—Melt granulated sugar over medium heat to brown syrup.

Chop—Cut in small pieces with knife, scissors, or chopper.

Combine—Mix ingredients.

Consommé—Clear broth made with meat and/or chicken.

Cream—Rub shortening against bowl with spoon or beat with mixer until light and creamy.

Cut in—Mix fat into flour mixture using a fork, two knives, or a pastry blender.

D

Dice—Cut into small cubes.

Dredge—Coat heavily with flour.

E

Entrée—Chief dish of the main course which is a meat, poultry, fish, or meat substitute.

Eclair—Oblong shape of cream puff paste filled with custard or whipped cream.

F

Filet—Boneless, thin strip of lean meat or fish.

Fold in—Cut down through, across bottom, up and over top, doing it over and over again until ingredients are blended.

French fry—Cook in hot

fat deep enough to float the food.

Fry—Panfry in small amount of fat.

G

Garnish—The extra that makes food look so good—a cherry or parsley.

Goulash—Thick Hungarian meat stew flavored with vegetables.

H

Hollandaise—Sauce made of butter and egg yolks with seasoning such as lemon juice or vinegar.

Hors d'oeuvres—Variety of delightful appetizers.

K

Knead—Work the dough with pressing, folding, and stretching motions. May also be pressing dough with heel of hand.

M

Marinate—Let food stand in dressing mixture (such as French) to give added flavor.

Meringue—Mixture of stiffly beaten egg whites and sugar—usually for pie topping.

Mince—Chop or cut into small pieces.

Mix—Stir ingredients together.

P

Pare—Cut away outside skin as from fruits and vegetables.

Peel—Strip off outside covering as from a banana.

Petits fours—Little iced cakes cut into fancy designs and frosted decoratively.

Pit—Take out seeds.

Poach—Cook by using simmering (not boiling) water or other liquid.

Preheat—Turning on oven in time for it to be at right temperature when you have food ready to put in.

R

Ravioli—Small shapes of Italian paste spread with meat or vegetable filling and folded over and cooked in meat stock.

Relish—Food that is highly flavored and used with other food.

S

Sauté—Brown in small amount of fat in skillet.

Scald—Heat milk to just below boiling point until you see tiny bubbles around the edges.

Sear—Brown surface quickly.

Simmer—Cook in liquid over very low heat. Bubbles are lazylike.

Stew—Cook slowly in small amount of liquid for long time.

Stir—Mix with a spoon.

T

Torte—Rich cake, usually made from crumbs, eggs, sugar, and nuts.

Tortilla—Thin round Mexican food made from cornmeal and hot water.

Toss—Lightly mix ingredients without mashing them.

W

Whip—Whipping adds air through rich cream or egg whites until light and fluffy. You simply beat rapidly.

IT'S TIME...

To Plan

The personal touch is delightful, whatever hobby you have. Your own homemade method of keeping recipes reflects your personality. Since it is such a versatile preoccupation, you will want to keep a record of recipes as you collect them. List the name of the person, magazine, or cookbook from which you got the recipe, and any special comments. It is a good practice to date the recipe and the times and places you served it. Another notation might include the comments of those who were served the dish.

Some women prefer file folders for their recipes. Others insist that the loose-leaf notebook is the best way to keep them. Bound notebooks have the vote of many because the pages are not so easily torn out. Perhaps the most popular way of keeping recipes is the card file. Three-by-five- or four-by-six-inch cards are used most frequently. They can be lifted out and posted before you as you work. Dividers for classification for meats, pastries, and so on make it easier to find the recipes.

When one of your recipes proves to be especially popular, you may receive requests for it. One way to give them to friends is by means of a personal recipe card.

IT'S TIME...

To Watch the Calories

Someone has said, "When you look into your mirror, the foods you ate yesterday will say 'hello' to you today." We tell our teenagers that it is just as important to have a correct pattern for their meals as for their dress. It is the *person* we see, regardless of how attractive the dress. Patterns may be altered and meals can be made to fit the needs of everyone in your family.

There is a difference in saying, "I'm not sick," and saying, "I feel wonderful." The difference may be in the nutritional savings account you have. This account improves body functions and stores reserves for emergencies. It applies to everything, except calories, and they have their own built-in saving account—five, twenty, sixty pounds of fat! Calories and activities must be balanced to maintain the normal weight we need.

Our family firmly believes in "breaking the fast." We know that the world looks brighter when we begin the day with a good breakfast, and it is entirely possible that we look brighter to the world! We need to look fit, and we can't if we have an energy lag from lack of breakfast.

It is fun to stay fit, and the right foods will help to do it. It may be a hard exercise—to push away from the table before you feel full, but it can prove to be a very good exercise. The mirror will reflect the radiant body and personality we *can* have by disciplined eating, *but it will not lie*.

IT'S TIME . . .

To Be Nosy

Yes, I said it's time to be "nosy" and know what is going on in your neighborhood. The next time there is an "occasion" like a brand-new baby, an anniversary, or return from a long vacation—why not send them something tasty to dine on? You'll be "neighbor of the day" to your friends. You can show your Christian concern this way.

Most families have illness or special diet problems sometime or another. The usual happy world takes on a less rosy look. Perhaps meals have to be served in bed. A regular bed tray is a good idea for those confined to bed. However, you can balance a tray on a pillow. It should be a very light pillow and large enough to hold the tray. You soon learn to keep hot food hot with heated dishes and cold foods cold with dishes chilled in the refrigerator before taking them to the patient. A fresh flower in scented water seems to perk up the spirits. But a surprise on the tray seems to please my patients most of all: a funny book, a new game, or just cutting the sandwiches into fancy shapes.

No matter how restricted the diet, it usually can be made tasty and attractive. Variety is important, but your happy manner will contribute just as much as the dish you take. A warm and reassuring manner is the best garnish of life. At any rate—be "nosy" and love your neighbors!

IT'S TIME . . .

To Be Special

Foods from far and near mirror the living conditions of people in various lands. We learn much about people when we study their foods as well as when we study their languages. Foods from foreign lands prove to be a challenge to the modern homemaker.

Perhaps in your neighborhood are people from other lands who would be flattered to show you how to make a native dish. Your meal could easily turn into a festive occasion with the use of a simple costume or table decoration. If you let the idea mushroom a little, you could have an international smorgasbord, with all of the guests bringing favorite dishes of foreign countries or of certain sections of the United States.

Mexican dishes of enchiladas, chili con carne, and tortillas are characterized by high seasoning. Often included in Mexican meals are avocado salads and cool fruit for dessert.

Chinese homemakers prepare food much in the manner of artists, carefully adding and blending in the flavors. Toppings of vegetables, meats, or fish usually cover the dish.

Japanese sukiyaki admittedly takes time to prepare, but is sheer artistry in flavor and delightful eating. An electric skillet permits the dish to be prepared at the table, and if you want the foreign atmosphere, sit on floor cushions to eat the meal.

Italian spaghetti and lasagna with their hearty meat sauces have earned acceptance around the world. Serve your favorite recipe with hard rolls or garlic bread and a crisp green salad. Rigatoni is a favorite for birthday dinners at our house.

French culinary art is enviable. Dining à la Paris is at its best when it is done in leisurely style. Onion soup, tossed salad with spicy dressing, and French bread or rolls will complement any main dish.

Scandinavian delicacies such as delectable Norwegian pancakes or Swedish meatballs are delightful for any meal. The meatballs are the basic entrée of most smorgasbords, and Finnish and Danish pastries have their own enviable reputation.

India's chicken curry with yellow rice is distinctive in flavor, and not difficult to make. It is a must for an international smorgasbord.

Austria is noted for the cake-like bread *gugelhupf*, which is often served for dessert. Bowls of stewed fruits make a nice companion for the bread.

Germany would not be Germany without its famous sauerbraten served with potato dumplings and sweet-sour red cabbage. The gingersnap gravy evokes many comments from those not familiar with this flavor.

United States regional dishes are a must for the table: Maryland beaten biscuits, Southern hush puppy, Boston baked beans, West Coast baked salmon, East Coast crab cakes, Baked Alaska, Hawaiian sweet potato balls, Louisiana boiled shrimp, and "everywhere" apple or cherry pie.

A festive touch for the meal would be to decorate cupcakes with tiny paper flags of the many nations. Background music could include recorded songs from other lands. Perhaps someone in the group could offer the table grace in another language.

IT'S TIME ...

To Talk

A table! What is a table? Forget that it is just a flat slab atop some legs. Rather, let's think that it is a companionable island where family and friends congregate to enjoy both the food and each other's company. It brings us together and stimulates the flow of conversation. It builds friendly lines of communication between strangers and extends the boundaries of our world in rich fellowship.

It's time now to think of the kind of table talk we share. May it be our determination to make our words enlightening, informative, and sharing. Martin Luther's *Table Talks* have become famous as a source of his thoughts and actions in the informal and relaxed atmosphere of his own dinner table. He frequently shared his correspondence with students gathered about the table. Even more important was his ministry to his own children while sitting at the table. By mingling theological discussions with the prattle of the children he gave deeper meaning to their increasing awareness of their father's mighty faith.

> . . . Call all our neighbors together,
> And when they appear,
> Let us make them such cheer
> As will keep out the wind and the weather.
> —Washington Irving.

IT'S TIME . . .

To Entertain

> Call a truce to our labors,
> Let us feast with friends and neighbors.
> —Rudyard Kipling

So you have an outside job and you can't entertain as much as you would like. Join the party! I know the feeling, too. With the help of a modern kitchen and many easily prepared foods, we *can* find time to have friends in for a snack or an occasional full-course dinner. I have been forced to find new and different ways to entertain. But I am determined to find time to share my table with my friends. Some simple ideas that have worked for me include—

Saturday morning breakfast for a few of the girl friends. This is a fun meal to plan, not too expensive, and a wonderful time to visit.

Dessert meeting right after lunch. Coffee and tea with a thin piece of dessert make a wonderful icebreaker or the topping for a meeting in your home.

Favorite dish meal for a few couples. The hostess acts as the leader and asks each couple to bring their favorite recipe dish. One brings the appetizer, another brings a salad, and the third couple brings a favorite dessert. The hostess serves the main dish. Expenses will be kept at a minimum—and so will the work!

Birthday party for the children. Rather than work too much on the games and prizes, I let the guests entertain themselves around the table—eating! Tiny hot dogs wrapped in "tube-prepared" biscuits always make a hit. They have a way of disappearing as fast as they come from the oven. With potato chips and baked beans, followed by the traditional cake and ice cream, we actually have a simple birthday meal.

Sunday night after-church snack provides a wonderful way to conclude the weekend with a few friends. Fancy cold cuts and unusual cheeses, rye bread with a mixed fruit or tossed salad—these are always welcome for the evening snack. You could climax it with some of your own homemade cookies; or a warm dessert would be a pleasant surprise for a winter evening. The main thing, though, is to keep it simple. You want to enjoy the company, so don't bog down in kitchen detail. Remember, the purpose of your entertaining is to share friendship, isn't it?

Teen-age "do it yourself" party. The ingredients for a pizza party include a large table and plenty of soft drinks mixed gently with several hungry teen-agers. This is all that you need for a wonderful climax to the basketball game, bowling party, or roller skating event. Individual pizzas may be made by rolling out the ready-to-bake tube biscuits. A variety of toppings may be ready for their individual orders. Dishes to clean up—none! Just use paper napkins to hold the pizza and have some straws for those who want them for the pop—or do you call it "soda" or "tonic" in your part of the country?

Neighborhood barbecue. Broiled hamburgers, hot dogs, or spareribs, mingled with the unique aroma that hickory-smoked wood or charcoal fire gives them, tell the neighbors, it is time to start meandering over to your backyard. Simple backyard buffet meals can be colorful and delicious, and easy on the cook. We have a tradition of making homemade ice cream for dessert for a new neighbor. It is not too hard to find someone to turn the crank so long as they know there are extra helpings to go around. For our purposes, I'm prejudiced *against* the electric type freezer!

You do not need a reason to entertain other than the sheer joy of doing it. For, "Cooking comes from the heart as well as the hearth."

And even though it's simple food—if you serve it with a happy frame of mind and a delightful spirit—it will be fit for a king—AMBROSIA!

IT'S TIME...

To Take Inventory

I saw an article the other day in which a teacher was telling of a time when she was depressed. The principal told her just to sit down and make a list of all the things her children liked about her. She tried it and it did wonders for her morale! Perhaps your list would look like this. What do people love you for?

MY FAMILY LIKES
... the way I tell them about when they were little.
... the way my eyes flash when they have forgotten to hang up their clothes.
... the way I laugh at their jokes at the dinner table.
... the way I let them decorate the Christmas tree.
... the way I sneeze off-key.
... the way I buy caramel corn after a shopping spree.
... the way *I* have matured as they get older.
... the way I love them even when they are not very lovable.
... the way I wear *their* favorite dress when I go out for dinner with my husband.
... the way I can alter the hand-me-downs from one to the other.
... the way I invite guests from the orphanage for holiday meals.
... the way I tell about the teen-age boys at high school.
... the way I tell them about their diseases and operations.

IT'S TIME...

To Keep Christmas

> A little child ... A shining star,
> A stable rude ... the door ajar.
> Yet in that place ... so crude, forlorn,
> The Hope of all ... the world was born.
> —Author unknown

May each home this Christmastime be filled with the spirit of Christmas joy and scented with the aroma of festive cooking. One of the outstanding pieces of literature for Christmas is this of Henry van Dyke's.

Are you willing to forget what you have done for other people, and to remember what other people have done for you; to ignore what the world owes you, and to think what you owe the world; to put your rights in the background, and your duties in the middle distance, and your chances to do a little more than your duty in the foreground; . . . to close your book of complaints against the management of the universe, and look around you for a place where you can sow a few seeds of happiness—are you willing to do these things even for a day? Then you can keep Christmas.

Are you willing to stoop down and consider the needs and the desires of little children; to remember the weakness and loneliness of people who are growing old; . . . to bear in mind the things that other people have to bear in their hearts; to try to understand what those who live in the same house with you really want, without waiting for them to tell you; to trim your lamp so that it will give more light and less smoke, and to carry it in front so that your shadow will fall behind you; to make a grave for your ugly thoughts and a garden for your kindly feelings, with the gate open—are you willing to do these things even for a day? Then you can keep Christmas.

Are you willing to believe that love is the strongest thing in the world—stronger than hate, stronger than evil, stronger than death—and that the blessed life which began in Bethlehem nineteen hundred years ago is the image and brightness of the Eternal Love? Then you can keep Christmas.

And if you keep it for a day, why not always?

But you can never keep it alone. . . .

—Henry van Dyke

IT'S TIME . . .

To Remember

The book and the television series "I Remember Mama" has triggered pleasant memories for many of us. It is good to have memories and good to share them as a part of building a Christian home.

I REMEMBER

... the hot biscuits, crisp bacon, and fried eggs that Mother made every morning. She still does, and to this day Dad doesn't think he is spoiled!

... the turnip greens that I detested, but they were made more palatable with Mother's good Southern corn bread.

... the "beaten" (with the side of a saucer) round steak, milk gravy, and brown biscuits we often had for supper. A pound of meat always seemed to stretch enough to be ample for everyone.

... the way Mother waited for me to get out of elementary school at noon so she could give me twenty cents. Ten cents was for a can of tomato soup and ten cents was for a half pound of marshmallow-cream-sandwich cookies which the clerk took out of a slanted bin.

... the way I had to wash and rinse all the pint and quart jars during the canning season. It was much easier to do them in the laundry tubs in the basement and carry them up to Mother who filled them with tomatoes, grape jam, pickles and peaches.

... company coming to our house and my having to wait for the second table. I guess we didn't know about buffet style serving.

... how mad I got when we had company and the teen-age boy took his second pork chop when there was only one each. Fortunately, Mother caught my eye before I told him what I thought!

... the way Mother would roll out the pie crust and deftly make a leaf design for the top crust.

... Mother beating egg whites for the meringue of the pie—and with a fork.

... Papa always saying the same grace:

> Grant us the blessing, Oh, Lord,
> For what we are about to receive,
> We humbly beg, for Christ's sake,   Amen.

(For years I thought he said, "We am the bag.")

... Papa expertly mixing sorghum and butter together. (My family tries this, but they are "sloppy" in their technique.)

... the way that green beans had to be cooked for hours with some meat seasonings. No undercooking was permitted—those beans couldn't fight back if they wanted to.

... the way Mother made a thin custard for fruit salad and put it in the same fruit bowl that graced her wedding table.

... the special treat of ice cream and ginger ale floats.

... the way I got to lick the frosting pan.

Ah, it's fun to remember!

IT'S TIME . . .

To Dig

> Of all the gifts I have each year,
> (Some sparkling, bright, and glowing)
> I think the gifts I hold most dear,
> Are ones so green and growing.
> —Author unknown

How hopeless the garden looks in the early spring. Winter damage for some plants is apparent by then, and we become convinced that many of the plants and shrubbery are dead. But patience might reveal that we should have had more faith. We uncover the base of our plants and pull away the mulch to let the warm rays of the sun get to the plants. Then we find that in what seemingly was dead there is new life eager for growing.

The important thing now is pruning. This cutting away of dead wood is necessary. And with the first flush of growth in the spring the pruning scars heal rapidly.

Springtime comes into our lives, too. We let prejudices take root. We let weeds of discontent spread. Our lives become stunted until the Master Gardener touches us with his healing strength. He knows what is best for us and we thrive only as we grow in him.

IT'S TIME . . .

To Perk Up

Nagging is almost an exclusively feminine characteristic. Few men use this weapon. It is a persistent sort of needling. It causes resentment and rebellion and often erases the husband's desire to please his wife. Perhaps the strongest argument against it is that it is habit forming. If it helps the wife get her way, she undoubtedly will resort to it again. Nagging heads the complaint list of unhappy husbands. It may win the immediate war, but it rarely wins lasting peace. Now if you really want to know how to treat your husband, here is just the recipe for you.

The first thing to do is catch him. But there's more to it—what you do with him afterward is important too. Many a good husband is spoiled by mismanagement. Some women go about it as if their husbands were balloons, and blow them up. Others keep them constantly in hot water. Others let them freeze by their carelessness and indifference. Some keep them in a stew by annoying words and ways. Some keep them in a pickle all their lives. Others roast them.

Now it is not supposed that any husband will be tender and good, managed in this way. But they are really delicious when properly treated. In selecting your husband, you should not be guided by the silvery appearance as when buying a mackerel, nor by the golden tint as if you wanted a salmon. Be sure to select him yourself, as tastes differ.

Next, obtain a preserving kettle or large jar, the finest to be had. See that the linen in which you wrap him is nicely washed and mended. Tie him in the kettle with the strong silken cord called "comfort," for the one called "duty" is often weak. If he sputters and sizzles, do not be anxious. Some husbands do this until they are quite done. Add a little sugar in the form of what confectioners call kisses. But please, no vinegar or pepper on any account. A little spice improves him, but it must be used with judgment. Never stick a sharp instrument into him to see if he is tender. You cannot fail to know when he is done.

Thus treated, you will find him reliable and good. He will usually agree with you and the children, and he will keep as long as you want him unless you become careless and set him into a cold place.

IT'S TIME . . .

To Hobo

Once again it is summer and we find the need for a change of pace as well as scenery. Said one busy mother after a long winter of busy activities:

> I feed the cat and feed the dog.
> I feed the cow, I feed the hog.
> I feed the kids, I feed the Turks;
> Some day I think I'll ditch the works!

We do need to look at something besides the kitchen stove and sink. We need firelight, moonlight, and sunlight! We need tramping and "lazing" around. We need to whiff the good wood smoke of a campfire. We need fun, food, and fellowship in the out-of-doors. We need to see the shimmer of a lake and to lean quietly against a tree. We need, too, to vocalize on or off key when the meal is over. Well, I guess we need it.

We will plan the "blue-sky" meals for simplicity and variety. We should avoid elaborateness or fanciness, but include colorful and attractive servings and the rule-of-thumb need for sweet and tart as well as both crisp and soft in the meal.

For successful "hoboing" you need to remember to:

. . . plan the menu and arrange for necessary equipment.
. . . bring the matches.
. . . use old pans.
. . . keep foods covered until needed.
. . . avoid easily perishable foods.
. . . be patient with the flies, ants, and other out-of-door insects.
. . . be a regular "Smokey the Bear" if you build a fire.
. . . have fun!

IT'S TIME...

To See Through Children's Eyes

Let's take time to look at life through our children's eyes. Their expressions are unique and their interpretations are often unusual. One mother I know makes it a hobby to keep many of the sayings of her children. She labels a manila folder for each child and in that folder files away each interesting remark and the date she heard it.

Through their minds some have expressed their thoughts this way:

Fingers are something you haff to have exactly ten of if you don't want to attrack attenshun. Fingers come in handy when you ferst lern to count with. Even after some people grow up they count better with their fingers than what they do with just their empty mind.

The *goose* is a low, heavy-set bird, composed most of meat and feathers. His head sets on one end and he sets on the other. There ain't no between of his toes. If I was a goose, I had rather be a gander.

A female *goat* is called a buttress; a little goat is called a goatee.

Husbands is a kind of fish, because I heard some ladies say that Miss Susie Jones was fishing for Mr. Brown. Husbands is the smartest people in the world and knows the most because they sit up all the evening and read the papers, and never waste any time talking to their wives.

A little *rabbit* is something like a cat except he has a powder puff where his tail ain't at!

IT'S TIME ...

To Color

October is out "painting the town." The gorgeous beauty of the autumn leaves compete with one another in their attempt to be more colorful. The vivid shades of color sparkle from limb to limb.

This reminds me of the adult coloring book idea which was recently popular. I thought it would be fun for us to try to color our lives a little brighter. Here are some of the people and things in my life I have colored. Why don't you try coloring some too?

HERE

... is my husband.....................Color him handsome.
... are my children....................Color them growing.
... are my relatives....................Color them sharing.
... is my home........................Color it cluttered.
... is my friend.......................Color her wonderful.
... is my friend faraway............Color her remembered.
... is the schoolteacher................Color her dedicated.
... is the restaurateur................Color him wife-saving.
... is the baker.......................Color him rising.
... is my budget.......................Color it strained.
... is my savings account.............Color it in the future.
... is the pastor......................Color him consecrated.
... is the church school...............Color it teaching.
... is my day.................Color it with new beginnings.
... is my week.........................Color it rushing.
... am I..Color me busy!

IT'S TIME ...

To Stew

Some do-it-yourself techniques for becoming completely miserable are these:

... Dwell on your own troubles.
... Always put yourself first.

... Nurse your grievances.
... Keep up with the neighbors.
... Talk constantly about your ailments.
... Always insist upon your own rights.

These techniques really work if you want to give enough time to them. Good luck—you'll need it!

Here is another way to say the same thing:

Trouble Cake

To ½ cup of disbelief in God's providence add 1 cup of self-rejection. Cream together until the resulting mixture resembles sour suspicion and a willingness to feel that the whole world has it in for you. Add 1 cup of conviction that ill health is necessary and exercise bad. Beat until the mixture thickens to inactivity. Sift together 1 teaspoon of resentment over the inevitable losses life brings, 2 teaspoons of refusal to try new things and adopt new interests, and 2½ cups of neglect of proper food, rest, and minor physical ailments. Add to the batter and beat well. Season with 1 teaspoon of fear for the future. Pour into the well-greased pan of hoarding the past, money, and possessions. Bake as long as desired in the oven of idleness.

Frost with self-pity. Place in the refrigerator of willed loneliness to ripen. Decorate with doubt that as long as we live we grow, and denial that each stage of life has its own limitations and its own rewards.

The result is a handsome lump of misery guaranteed to make your nineties a burden and yourself a worry to all around you.—Ina May Greer, 3 Arlington St., Boston, Mass.

IT'S TIME . . .

To Portray

Have you had your picture taken recently? In the fall we begin to think of Christmas and the gifts we can give. Pictures are high on the list. How did you pose for your last picture? How did you appear to others? Yes, how *do* others see you in your everyday life? To your *family* you might be the one who

. . . is always telling me to be quiet.
. . . is always telling me to hurry.
. . . frowns when she looks in my room and says it needs cleaning up *now*.
. . . is always insisting that I am too young, but I'm not!
. . . is "certainly changing in the last year."
. . . is uncanny—how can you make the car start by just straightening the license plate?

To the *world*—the paper boy, clerk, dentist, milkman, P.T.A.—you might be the one who is poised, patient, kind, humble, and honest.

To *friends*—next-door neighbor, club group, best friend—you might be the one who is gracious, gay, good conversationalist, and has a rich mind.

To *God*—who knows us best—we portray that which we really are—no pretense or sham is permitted.

So go ahead and pose, for you are lovely. The loveliness of the woman is in her expression, both words and action. The best part of beauty is that which no picture can express.

IT'S TIME . . .

To Season

Summer is over. Activities begin to gain momentum. Perhaps this is the best time to take stock of ourselves and see if the seasoning in our own lives is all that it should be. How do you stand?

DO YOU

... get adequate rest and sleep?
... Consider your family your No. 1 job? Add to your husband's stature in looking after him?
... cultivate recreational activities and hobbies?
... get away from the family briefly and devote some time to your own interests?
... help in community jobs: P.T.A., collection of funds?
... forget criticism and do jobs that are in the bounds of your strength?
... know that even a good job has some monotony? What is yours?
... analyze those things that irk you? Most of the things are not worth the expenditure of emotion.
... refuse to carry over anxieties from one day to the next? Rest them at the end of the day.
... keep growing intellectually? Don't rest on your husband's laurels.
... express the mind and the conviction that is yours?
... love those persons with whom you work in spite of their faults?
... attempt to be teachable?
... try to be yourself?

If you can do these things, you are growing up. You have traded illusion for reality. You have the power to rule the world, but must learn the strength of the meek. Your vocal knowledge must sometimes stand behind silent wisdom.

IT'S TIME . . .

To Devote

Here is a recipe for Christian living that I thought you would enjoy. It is really just casting our bread upon the waters, isn't it?

Recipe for Christian Living

Blend 1 cup of *Love* with
   ½ cup of *Kindness;*
Alternately add in small portions:
   1 cup of *Appreciation* and
   3 cups of *Pleasant Companionship*
Into which has been sifted
   2 teaspoons of *Deserving Praise.*
Flavor with 1 teaspoon of *Carefully Chosen Advice.*
Lightly fold in 1 cup of *Cheerfulness,* to which has been added a pinch of *Sorrow;*
Pour with *Tender Care* into *Clean Hearts* and let bake until well matured.
Turn out on the *Surface of Society;*
Humbly invoke *God's Blessing,* and it will *Serve all Mankind.*

—Anonymous

FOR RECIPES
Beverages

Some like them hot and some like them cold!

For *timesaving tips* use the frozen fruit juice concentrates, ready-to-serve eggnog, instant cocoa or hot chocolate milk. For the *extra special touch* use molds for freezing colored water, ginger ale or water with maraschino cherries or fruit slices. Place the mold with the fruit side up in the punch bowl. Fruit juice "ice cubes" are pretty, especially when mint leaves are frozen into the juice.

Fruit Punch

6 cups of fruit juices—pineapple, orange, lemon or lime
3 cups sugar
9 cups water
1 quart ginger ale
1½ quarts sherbet or ice cream

Boil sugar and 4 cups water to dissolve sugar. Cool. Add fruit juice and remaining water. Chill. After putting it in the punch bowl, add the ginger ale and top with scoops of sherbet. Makes 6 quarts or 48 punch-cup size servings.

Confetti Punch

2 cups orange juice
½ cup lemon juice
3½ cups pineapple juice
1 quart ginger ale
lemon sherbet
Gumdrops, finely cut

Mix and pour chilled fruit juices into punch bowl. Add chilled ginger ale. Float scoops of lemon sherbet on punch and dot the sherbet with finely cut gumdrops.

Citrus Punch

- 1 6-ounce can frozen orange juice
- 1 6-ounce can frozen lemonade
- 1 6-ounce can frozen limeade
- 1 quart cold water
- 1 quart ginger ale

Combine all ingredients except ginger ale. Pour over ice block or cubes in bowl. Add ginger ale just before serving. Garnish with mint leaves if desired. Makes 12 to 15 servings. Double the recipe to fill large punch bowl.

Party Punch

To satisfy guests, place 4 tea bags in 1 quart boiling water, steep 10 minutes. Cool. Add 1 quart ginger ale, 1 large can pineapple juice, 1 large can orange juice. Sweeten to taste with brown sugar, white sugar, or white syrup.

Orange Punch

Wash and cut 6 oranges. Squeeze juice and set aside. Grind rinds. Pour 2 quarts of boiling water over rinds, and let cool. Add 1 ounce of citric acid to orange juice. Drain liquid from rinds and to it add orange juice. Stir in 5 pounds sugar. Add a large can pineapple juice. Makes about 5 quarts of syrup. To each quart of syrup, add 4 quarts of water.

Pink and White Cherry Punch

Mix 2 quarts cold milk with ½ teaspoon almond extract and ½ cup maraschino cherry syrup. Add 1 quart of cherry-vanilla ice cream or 1 cup chopped maraschino cherries with vanilla ice cream.

Hot Minted Chocolate

Add 8 to 12 chocolate peppermint patties to 1 quart of scalded milk.

Hot Spiced Tomato Juice

Add 2 beef bouillon cubes, 1 tablespoon lemon juice, and ½ teaspoon Worcestershire sauce to 5 cups heated tomato juice.

▲ ▲ ▲

*The clouds have a silver lining—
   don't forget;
And though he's hidden, still the
   sun is shining;
Courage! instead of tears and vain
   repining
Just bide a wee and dinna fret.*
   —*Anonymous*

▼ ▼ ▼

Breads

(Rolls, Buns, Pancakes)

The simplest meal is given a delightful lift with homemade bread. Yeast rolls, either plain or sweet, are no trick to make; with a good basic yeast dough recipe many adaptations may be made. Any effort on your part will be well worth it in the words of praise you will receive.

Yeast Bread Recipe for Rolls, Buns, or Coffee Cake

- 2 cakes yeast
- 3 tablespoons lard
- 1 tablespoon butter
- 1 cup lukewarm water
- 1¼ teaspoons salt
- 4 tablespoons sugar
- 1 pint warm milk
- Approximately 2 pounds flour

Soften yeast in 1 cup of lukewarm water. Scald milk (1 pint); add sugar, salt, lard, and butter—all mixed together. Then add dissolved yeast to flour and mix well by kneading until smooth and elastic. Place in lightly greased bowl, cover with cloth and let rise in a warm place (75° to 95°) until double in bulk, about 2 hours. Punch down and form into shape desired. Place on greased baking sheets, 1½ inches apart. Let rise again in warm place until double in bulk. Bake 15 to 20 minutes in hot oven at 400°.

▲ ▲ ▲

Love moves toward others; fear shrinks from others.

▼ ▼ ▼

Refrigerator Rolls

1 cake yeast
2 tablespoons lukewarm water
½ cup sugar
2 cups scalded milk (cooled to lukewarm)
2 beaten eggs
1 teaspoon salt
6 cups flour
¾ cup melted shortening, lukewarm

Dissolve yeast and sugar in 2 tablespoons of lukewarm water. Mix in the milk, eggs, and salt. Add part of flour—do not knead. Add melted shortening and mix well. Add rest of flour; mix until smooth.

Cover and let stand in refrigerator overnight. Take out. Roll in thirds (not too thin). Cut into 12 wedges. Put wedges on greased cookie sheet. Let stand 3 hours in a warm place. Bake 15 minutes at 425°. (When rolling, start at outer edge and roll toward center.)

Soft Molasses Bread

1 cup molasses
½ cup butter and shortening mixed
1 cup sour milk or coffee
2 teaspoons baking soda
1 cup sugar
2 eggs
3 cups sifted flour
½ teaspoon ginger
¼ teaspoon cinnamon
¼ teaspoon cloves
¼ teaspoon nutmeg

Cream butter and sugar. Add eggs, molasses, and rest of ingredients. Add soda, dissolved first in a little warm water. Bake in 9-inch square tins. Bake in moderate oven because molasses burns easily.

▲ ▲ ▲

"I do not know how the great loving Father will bring out light at last, but He knows, and He will do it."

—*David Livingstone*

▼ ▼ ▼

Sour Cream Biscuits

2 cups flour
½ teaspoon salt
2½ teaspoons baking powder
½ teaspoon soda
2 tablespoons butter
¾ cup thick sour cream

Sift together the flour, salt, baking powder, and soda. Work in butter with tips of fingers or knife. Add sour cream and stir quickly and vigorously until it thickens. Press or roll to ½- to ¾-inch thickness. Brush tops with milk. Bake in hot oven (425°) for about 12 minutes or until crust is browned evenly.

Nut Bread

4 cups flour
4 teaspoons baking powder
1 teaspoon salt
1 egg
1½ cups milk
1 cup walnuts
1 cup sugar

Combine all dry ingredients; then beat egg and milk together. Add to the dry ingredients. Bake in a bread pan which has been well greased. Let set in a warm room ½ hour; then bake for 1 hour at 350°.

Banana Bread

½ cup shortening
2 eggs
2 cups flour
1 teaspoon salt
½ teaspoon vanilla
1 cup sugar
1½ cups mashed bananas (3 large ones)
1 teaspoon soda
⅔ cup chopped nuts

Cream shortening and sugar. Add beaten eggs, mix well. Add bananas. Add dry ingredients, vanilla, and nuts. Makes two small loaves. Put in greased pans and bake one hour at 300° to 325°. Use plain or iced.

Health Bran Bread

1 cake dry yeast
3 cups lukewarm water
2 cups all-bran cereal
1 teaspoon salt
½ cup blackstrap molasses
2 tablespoons shortening
5 or 6 cups sifted flour

Dissolve 1 cake of yeast or 1 package of dry yeast in 3 cups lukewarm water; then add all-bran cereal, scant teaspoon salt, blackstrap molasses, and shortening. When bran is dissolved, add all-purpose sifted flour. Knead well. Set aside to rise about 2 hours; knead again. Make into 2 loaves; let rise again until it rebounds when pressed with the tip of finger. Bake 40 to 50 minutes in oven preheated to 400°. You can vary heat more or less. Loaves will weigh 2 pounds. If you don't want loaves that heavy, make into three loaves and bake less time.

Bran Muffins

1 cup all-bran cereal
¾ cup milk
1 egg
¼ cup soft shortening
1 cup sifted flour
2½ teaspoons baking powder
½ teaspoon salt
¼ cup sugar

Combine bran and milk. Let stand until most of moisture is taken up. Add egg and shortening and beat well.

In second bowl sift together flour, baking powder, salt, and sugar. Add to first mixture, stirring only until combined. Fill greased muffin pans ⅔ full. Bake in moderate oven (375°) about 30 minutes. If sour milk or buttermilk is used, reduce baking powder to 1 teaspoon and add ½ teaspoon baking soda.

Light Date and Nut Bread

1½ cups boiling water
1 cup chopped pitted dates
¾ cup granulated sugar
1 egg, beaten
2¼ cups sifted flour
Salt
¼ teaspoon baking powder
2 teaspoons baking soda
1 cup chopped walnuts
1 tablespoon melted shortening
1 teaspoon vanilla

Pour boiling water over dates. Let stand 10 minutes. Meanwhile add sugar and egg. Sift flour and add baking powder, salt, and soda. Stir in walnuts; add date mixture. Stir in shortening and add vanilla. Pour in greased loaf pan. Bake in moderate oven (350°) for 1 hour and 15 minutes.

Applesauce Muffins

1¼ cups flour
3 teaspoons baking powder
½ teaspoon salt
2 tablespoons sugar
1 cup all-bran cereal
1 beaten egg
⅓ cup milk
⅔ cup applesauce
¼ cup melted shortening

Sift together the flour, baking powder, salt, and sugar; blend in all-bran cereal. In another bowl blend: beaten egg, milk, applesauce, and shortening. Mix all ingredients and fill greased muffin tins ⅔ full. Bake 20 minutes at 400°. Makes 12 muffins.

▲ ▲ ▲

Four things a man must learn to do
If he would make his record true:
    To think, without confusion, clearly;
    To act, from honest motives, purely;
    To love his fellow man sincerely,
    To trust in God and heaven securely.
                            —Henry van Dyke

▼ ▼ ▼

Dumplings

1 cup flour	½ cup fine, dry bread crumbs
2 teaspoons baking powder	1 beaten egg
1 teaspoon salt	⅔ cup milk
2 tablespoons butter	2 teaspoons grated onion

Sift together the flour, baking powder, and salt; then cut in butter. Add bread crumbs. Blend in 1 beaten egg, milk, and grated onion. Mix only until moistened. Drop batter onto hot liquid. These dumplings are particularly good on beef stew. Cover and steam for 20 minutes.

Blueberry Muffins

¾ cup sugar	2 teaspoons baking powder
½ cup shortening (part butter)	½ teaspoon salt
2 eggs, separated	1 cup milk
2⅓ cups flour	1 cup blueberries

Cream sugar and shortening together. Add egg yolks and mix well. Add baking powder and salt to flour and stir to blend. Set aside ½ cup of blended dry ingredients. Add remaining dry ingredients, alternately with milk, to creamed mixture. Beat egg whites until stiff, and fold into batter. Dredge the blueberries in ½ cup of blended dry ingredients, and fold mixture into batter. Fill greased muffin cups ⅔ full. Bake for 20 to 25 minutes at 400°.

▲ ▲ ▲

The bamboo tree stands for prosperity. The pine tree means long life. The plum tree suggests courage because it puts out its blossoms while the snow is still on the ground.

▼ ▼ ▼

Sweet Potato Biscuits

1¼ cups flour
4 teaspoons baking powder
½ teaspoon salt
1 tablespoon sugar
¾ cup mashed sweet
  potatoes (cold)
⅔ cup milk
4 tablespoons melted
  butter or shortening

Mix together flour, baking powder, salt, and sugar. Add remaining ingredients, mixed together. Toss the soft dough on a heavily floured board. Flatten and cut with biscuit cutter. Place on greased baking pan and bake 15 minutes in 425° oven. Makes about 2 dozen small biscuits.

Blueberry Buckle

½ cup shortening
1 well-beaten egg
2½ teaspoons baking
  powder
½ cup milk
2 cups fresh blueberries or
  drained canned blue-
  berries
½ cup sugar
2 cups sifted enriched flour
¼ teaspoon salt
. . .
½ cup sugar
½ cup sifted enriched
  flour
½ teaspoon cinnamon
¼ cup butter or
  margarine

Thoroughly cream shortening and ½ cup sugar; add egg and mix well. Sift 2 cups flour, baking powder, and salt; add to creamed mixture, alternately with milk. Pour into a well-greased 11½ x 7½ x 1½-inch pan; sprinkle blueberries over batter. Combine ½ cup sugar, ½ cup flour, cinnamon and butter till crumbly; sprinkle over blueberries. Bake in moderate oven at 350° 45 to 50 minutes. Cut in squares and serve warm.

Butterscotch Rolls

2¼ cups milk	2 eggs, beaten
2 yeast cakes	About 7 cups flour
¼ cup sugar (heavy)	1 cup light brown sugar
2½ teaspoons salt	¼ cup butter
½ cup shortening	Cinnamon

Scald milk and melt shortening in it as it cools. Mix sugar and yeast until it liquifies. When milk is lukewarm, add to yeast and sugar. Add beaten eggs and beat in flour and salt until you have a soft dough. Sprinkle with flour and pat into a ball in the mixing bowl. Cover and set bowl in the ice box until three hours before needed.

Generously grease muffin tins, being sure to grease them heavily. For every dozen rolls, mix 1 cup light brown sugar with ¼ cup butter and put a spoonful in bottom of each section of muffin tin. Now roll the dough into an oblong shape about ¼ inch thick. Spread with melted butter and sprinkle with cinnamon. Roll into a long roll and cut into pieces about one inch thick. Place in muffin tin and let rise in a warm room 2 to 3 hours, or until double in bulk. Bake in 400° oven about 25 minutes. Be careful that the sugar does not burn. Before removing them from the oven, have a large flat pan ready and turn the tin over immediately onto this. Lift and let sugar run onto the rolls. Don't burn your fingers! This recipe makes about 4 dozen and can be kept in refrigerator several days and made into rolls as desired.

Norwegian Pancakes

1 cup flour
¼ teaspoon salt
1 tablespoon melted butter
1 teaspoon vanilla or lemon extract
1 tablespoon sugar
3 eggs, separated
2 cups milk

Sift flour, salt, and sugar together. Beat egg yolks; add milk and flavoring. Next, add flour mixture and melted butter. Last, fold in stiffly beaten egg whites. Put small amount of batter in hot greased skillet and tip skillet until batter covers entire surface. Turn when light tan on one side; cook other side. Take out and roll like little log. To serve, unroll, smear with butter, and sprinkle generously with powdered sugar; then reroll and eat. Not for calorie-conscious people.

Corn Bread

1 cup flour
1 cup yellow cornmeal
4 teaspoons baking powder
½ teaspoon salt
½ cup sugar
1 egg
1 cup milk
½ cup soft shortening

Sift dry ingredients into a medium bowl. Add milk, egg, and shortening. Beat with egg beater 1 minute. Don't overbeat. Bake 20 to 25 minutes at 425°.

Potato Pancakes

3 grated white potatoes, raw
2 eggs
1 tablespoon grated onion
1 tablespoon baking powder
2 tablespoons flour
1 teaspoon salt
¼ cup milk

Mix all ingredients and drop by tablespoonfuls on well-greased griddle. Bake approximately 3 minutes on each side.

Cakes

1—2—3—4—Cake

1 cup butter or margarine (½ pound)
2 cups sugar
3 cups flour
4 eggs
2 teaspoons vanilla
2 teaspoons baking powder
¼ teaspoon salt
1 cup milk

Thoroughly cream butter and sugar; add eggs, one at a time, beating after each addition. Add sifted dry ingredients, alternately with milk. Add vanilla. Bake in tube pan at 375° for 35 minutes. Test with toothpick or cake tester. You can make this cake in 9-inch layer cake pan for chocolate or coconut cake.

Pound Cake

½ pound butter
1 pound sugar
4 eggs
1 cup milk
3 cups flour
1 teaspoon vanilla
1 teaspoon baking powder
1 teaspoon salt
Nuts

Have everything at room temperature. Cream soft butter; add sugar and mix well together. Add cold eggs one at a time, mixing well. Sift flour three times with salt and baking powder. Add vanilla to milk. Add flour, then milk, alternately, until well mixed. Bake 1 hour or until golden brown at 350°. Nuts may be floured and added for extra flavor.

▲ ▲ ▲

The language of friendship is not words, but meanings. It is an intelligence above language.

▼ ▼ ▼

Cinnamon Cake

3 eggs
1½ cups sugar
¾ cup milk
2 cups sifted flour
2 teaspoons baking powder
4 tablespoons melted butter

Beat eggs until light. Add sugar slowly. Fold in dry ingredients, alternately with the milk. Add melted butter and blend thoroughly. Pour into a greased 13x9-inch pan. Sprinkle 5 tablespoons of melted butter on top. Blend ½ cup sugar with 2 teaspoons cinnamon. Sprinkle on top of cake. Bake in a 400° oven for 25 to 30 minutes.

Devil's Food Cake

2 cups sifted cake flour
2 cups sugar
½ cup shortening
3 squares melted chocolate
1¼ cups buttermilk or sour milk
1 teaspoon salt
1½ teaspoons baking soda
½ teaspoon baking powder
3 eggs
1 teaspoon vanilla

Put sifted cake flour, sugar, shortening, melted chocolate, ¾ cup milk (buttermilk or sour), and salt into mixer. Mix thoroughly by hand or medium speed of electric mixer for 2 minutes. Stir in baking soda and baking powder. Add ½ cup buttermilk or sour milk, eggs, and vanilla. Mix thoroughly and bake in 2 deep, 9-inch cake pans (1½ inches deep). Bake about 40 minutes at 350°.

▲ ▲ ▲

Time is the great equalizer. The same amount is given to the great as to the small—to the young as to the old. The difference lies in the way time is used.

▼ ▼ ▼

Cheese Cake

3 cups crushed graham crackers
¼ pound butter or margarine, melted
3 8-ounce packages cream cheese
4 eggs
1 teaspoon vanilla
1 cup sugar

Combine graham crackers and margarine; press firmly into bottom of 9-inch angel food pan (or your choice of other containers) to form crust.

Combine cheese, eggs, vanilla, and sugar; beat together well. Pour into pan over crumb crust. Bake in 350° oven for 30 minutes. Cool 15 minutes.

Topping: Combine 1 pint sour cream, 4 tablespoons sugar, and 1 teaspoon vanilla. Pour over top of partially cooled cheesecake and return to 350° oven for 15 additional minutes. Cool and refrigerate overnight. Freeze any unused portion. This recipe serves 20.

Danish Apple Cake

1 box Holland Rusk (crushed)
¼ pound butter
1 quart applesauce
1 teaspoon cinnamon
Sugar to taste

Put Rusk and butter in frying pan and lightly brown together. Combine applesauce, cinnamon, and sugar.

Spoon 1 layer of Rusk on bottom of pie plate. Cover this with a layer of the apple mixture. Continue in layers until dish is almost filled (end with Rusk layer). Serve with whipping cream spread over the entire top.

▲ ▲ ▲

"Often our severest tensions arise because we demand our loved ones to be perfect."

▼ ▼ ▼

Banana Cake

1½ cups sugar	5 tablespoons buttermilk
⅔ cup shortening	1 teaspoon vanilla
2 eggs	2 cups flour
1 cup mashed bananas	1 teaspoon soda
½ teaspoon salt	1 teaspoon baking powder

Cream sugar and shortening; add slightly beaten eggs. Sift dry ingredients and add alternately with milk. Add bananas and blend. Bake in round, greased and floured pans at 350°.

Topping: Prepare while cake is baking. Cook to the consistency of caramel: 10 tablespoons brown sugar, 6 tablespoons melted butter, and ¼ cup milk. Remove from heat and add 1 cup of nutmeats and 1 cup coconut. Spread on cake while cake is hot. Place under broiler until topping bubbles.

Hot Milk Sponge Cake

4 eggs	¼ teaspoon salt
2 cups sugar	2 tablespoons butter or margarine
2 teaspoons vanilla	1 cup hot milk
2 cups all-purpose flour	
2 teaspoons baking powder	

Beat eggs until light and thick; gradually add sugar and continue beating. Add vanilla. Fold sifted dry ingredients into egg mixture. Melt butter in hot milk and add all at one time. Pour into two greased 8-inch square or two 9-inch round pans and bake at 375° for 30 to 35 minutes. You may use a tube pan or make two upside-down cakes.

▲ ▲ ▲

"All sunshine makes the desert."
—*Arabian proverb*

▼ ▼ ▼

Apple Cake

2 cups sugar
1½ cups liquid shortening
3 cups flour
1 teaspoon cinnamon
3 cups diced apples
1 cup chopped nuts
2 beaten eggs
1 teaspoon almond extract
1 teaspoon soda
1 teaspoon salt

Combine sugar, shortening, eggs, and flavoring. Sift together dry ingredients; blend into first mixture. Fold in apples and nuts. Grease and flour oblong cake pan. Bake 45 minutes at 350°.

Lazy Daisy Cake

1 tablespoon margarine
½ cup milk
. . .
2 eggs
1 cup sugar
1 cup flour
¼ teaspoon baking powder
. . .
1 teaspoon baking powder

Heat together the margarine and milk. Set aside. Combine 2 eggs and 1 cup sugar; beat well. Sift together the flour and ¼ teaspoon baking powder, and add to eggs and sugar. Mix well, then add hot milk and margarine gradually. Put in 1 teaspoon baking powder last. Bake in 325° oven about 35 minutes. Use 8x12-inch pan.

Topping: Melt together 3 tablespoons butter, 5 tablespoons brown sugar, 2 tablespoons cream. Add ¾ cup coconut. When cake is done, spread this on top while it is hot; place under broiler to toast. Watch carefully, for it burns easily.

▲ ▲ ▲

"Don't waste five-dollar time on a five-cent job." —*John T. Faris*

▼ ▼ ▼

Prune Cake

- ½ cup shortening
- 1 cup sugar
- 2 eggs
- 1½ cups cake flour
- ½ teaspoon salt
- ½ teaspoon baking soda
- ½ teaspoon baking powder
- ½ teaspoon cinnamon
- ½ teaspoon cloves
- ½ teaspoon nutmeg
- ⅔ cup sour milk
- ⅔ cup cooked prune pieces

Cream shortening and sugar together. Add eggs, beating after each addition. Sift dry ingredients and add alternately with milk, stirring until blended. Fold in prunes. Pour batter into two greased and floured 8-inch round cake pans. Bake for 35 minutes at 350°.

Frosting: Blend 3 tablespoons butter with ¼ cup hot prune juice, 1 teaspoon vanilla, and ½ teaspoon lemon extract. Beat in 2 tablespoons chopped prunes and ½ cup chopped nuts. Gradually add about 2 cups sifted confectioners' sugar, beating until mixture is smooth and of spreading consistency. Spread on cake when cooled.

White Fruit Cake

- 5 large eggs
- ½ pound butter or substitute
- 1 cup granulated sugar
- 1¾ cups all-purpose flour
- ½ teaspoon baking powder
- ¾ pound cherries
- 1 pound pineapple
- 1 quart pecans
- ½ ounce pure lemon extract

Cream butter and sugar; add beaten eggs. Chop nuts and fruit in medium pieces; mix with part of flour. Sift remainder flour and baking powder. Fold into eggs and butter, add flavoring. Put into greased, paper-lined pan. Place in cold oven. Bake at 250° for 3 hours. Cool in pan on cake rack.

Fresh Coconut Cake

- ¼ pound butter
- 3 eggs
- 2 cups cake flour
- 1 teaspoon flavoring (any kind)
- Grated coconut
- 1½ cups sugar
- 1 cup milk
- 3 teaspoons baking powder
- 1 teaspoon salt

Cream butter, eggs, and sugar. Sift flour, salt, and baking powder together. Add alternately with milk, to creamed mixture. Add flavoring. Bake in 350° oven 25 to 30 minutes. Frost with seven-minute icing, using two egg whites. Use fresh grated coconut for topping.

English Fruit Cake

- 1 cup shortening
- 1 cup brown sugar
- 6 eggs
- ¼ cup grape juice
- ¼ cup lemon juice
- ¼ cup orange juice
- 2½ cups sifted cake flour
- 2 teaspoons baking powder
- ½ teaspoon soda
- ½ teaspoon mace
- 1 teaspoon allspice
- 1½ teaspoons cinnamon
- ¾ teaspoon salt
- 1 pound raisins
- 1 pound currants
- ½ pound candied citron
- ¼ pound candied lemon peel
- ¼ pound candied orange peel
- ½ pound figs
- ½ pound pitted dates
- ½ cup candied cherries
- ½ cup candied pineapple
- ¼ pound blanched, cut almonds

Cream shortening and sugar, add well-beaten eggs and beat thoroughly. Add sifted dry ingredients, alternately with fruit juices. Fold in fruit, almonds, and peel. Pour into paper lined, oiled pans. Bake at 275° to 300° for about 2½ to 3 hours. Makes two 3½-pound cakes.

Quick Cocoa Cakes

1 cup sugar
1 egg
½ cup cocoa
½ cup shortening
½ cup milk
1 teaspoon soda
¾ teaspoon salt
1½ cups flour
½ cup boiling water

Put all ingredients together and beat about 3 minutes. Fill cups about half full. Bake 25 minutes at 350°. Makes 18 cup cakes.

Perfect Yellow Cake

3 cups sifted cake flour
½ teaspoon salt
1 teaspoon vanilla
2 cups sugar
¾ cup milk
3 teaspoons baking powder
1 cup butter, margarine or shortening (½ pound)
4 eggs

Grease bottoms and sides of pans with unsalted fat and flour. Measure flour, sift first. Then sift with salt and baking powder. Cream the shortening thoroughly until fluffy, then gradually add sugar and cream until it looks like whipped cream. Add eggs, one at a time, unbeaten; beat very hard after each egg; add vanilla or any other flavoring you wish. Add flour and milk alternately, starting with flour and ending with flour. Makes 3 8-inch layers or 2 9-inch layers. Bake 25 to 30 minutes at 375°.

▲ ▲ ▲

"Instead of allowing yourself to be so unhappy, just let your love grow as God wants it to grow; seek goodness in others, love more persons more; love them more impersonally, more unselfishly, without thought of return. The return, never fear, will take care of itself."
—*Henry Drummond*

▼ ▼ ▼

Ice-Cream Cake

½ cup butter	2 cups sugar
1 cup water	2½ cups flour
½ cup cornstarch	2 teaspoons baking powder
4 egg whites	1½ teaspoons vanilla

Cream butter and sugar. Add a little water. Sift flour, cornstarch, and baking powder together and add to butter mixture, alternately with water. Mix to a smooth batter. Flavor and fold in egg whites which have been beaten. Bake in a moderate oven. Use marshmallow or coconut icing.

Two-Egg Treasure Cake

2 cups sifted cake flour	½ cup shortening
1⅓ cups sugar	1 cup less 2 tablespoons milk
2½ teaspoons baking powder	1½ teaspoons vanilla
1 teaspoon salt	2 eggs, unbeaten

Sift dry ingredients into mixing bowl. Drop in shortening. Add ⅔ of milk, then vanilla, and beat for 2 minutes on low speed of mixer. Add eggs and remaining milk and beat additional 2 minutes. Bake in 2 8-inch round layer pans at 375° oven for 25 to 35 minutes. Frost with chocolate frosting.

Gingerbread

½ cup shortening	2½ cups flour
½ cup sugar	1½ teaspoons baking soda
½ teaspoon salt	1 teaspoon ginger
1 cup molasses	1 cup boiling coffee

Cream shortening and add sugar; then sift and add flour and ginger. Mix in molasses and boiling coffee, to which has been added the baking soda. Beat enough to mix thoroughly, pour into well-greased pan. Bake at 350° for 40 to 50 minutes. White frosting can be used if desired.

Applesauce Cake

1½ cups applesauce (1 can)
2 tablespoons cocoa
1 cup sugar
1 cup raisins
½ cup shortening, melted
2 cups flour
1 teaspoon cinnamon
½ teaspoon cloves
½ teaspoon allspice
½ teaspoon salt
2 teaspoons soda

Put sugar, raisins, spices, salt, and cocoa in applesauce. Stir well. Add melted shortening, then flour which has been sifted with the soda. Bake in 8-inch square pan at 350° for one hour, or until done.

Chocolate Nut Torte

5 eggs
2½ cups sugar
1 tablespoon butter
1¼ cups milk, scalded
2½ cups cake flour
⅛ teaspoon salt
2½ teaspoons baking powder
1 teaspoon vanilla

Beat eggs until light. Gradually add 1 cup sugar and beat until light colored and fluffy. Combine milk and butter; gradually add to egg mixture. Add sifted dry ingredients and vanilla. Mix well. Bake in 2 wax paper-lined 9-inch layer pans at 350°. Baking time: 30 minutes. Cool. Cut layers in half.

▲ ▲ ▲

He who knows not, and knows not that he knows not, is a fool, shun him;
He who knows not, and knows that he knows not, is a child, teach him.
He who knows, and knows not that he knows, is asleep, wake him.
He who knows, and knows that he knows, is wise, follow him.

—*Persian proverb*

▼ ▼ ▼

Frosting

- 2 cups milk
- ½ cup granulated sugar
- ½ cup enriched flour
- ¼ cup cocoa
- ⅓ cup milk (cold)
- 1 cup butter
- 1 cup confectioner's sugar
- 2 teaspoons vanilla
- 1½ cups chopped English walnuts

Heat 2 cups milk in a double boiler. Combine granulated sugar, flour, cocoa, and ⅓ cup cold milk. Add to hot milk and cook over hot water until thickened, about 20 minutes, stirring constantly. Remove from heat, cover, cool to room temperature. Thoroughly cream butter and confectioners' sugar. Add to cooked, *cooled* mixture. Add vanilla. Beat smooth. Spread between layers (4), and on top and sides. Sprinkle nuts on top to decorate.

Butterscotch Chewy Cake

- 4 medium eggs
- 2 cups brown sugar
- 1 tablespoon butter
- 1½ cups sifted flour
- 1½ teaspoons baking powder
- . . .
- 1½ cups nuts
- 1 teaspoon vanilla

Beat eggs with rotary beater in top of double boiler until blended. Blend in brown sugar and butter. Place over rapidly boiling water, stirring constantly until hot, about 5 minutes. Remove from heat.

Sift together sifted flour and baking powder. Add all at once to cooked mixture; mix until well blended. Stir in chopped pecans or other nuts and vanilla. Turn into well-greased and lightly floured 13x9-inch pan. Bake in moderate oven, 350°, 25 to 30 minutes or until it springs back when touched lightly with finger tips. Serve with ice cream or whipped cream or sprinkle while warm with sifted confectioners' sugar.

Creamy Caramel Icing

For large cake:
⅓ cup cream
6 tablespoons butter
2 tablespoons sugar
3 cups confectioner's sugar

For small cake:
¼ cup
4½ tablespoons
2 tablespoons
2¼ cups

Heat together cream and butter. Meanwhile caramelize 2 tablespoons sugar. Add scalded cream and butter, stirring until lumps are dissolved. Gradually stir in confectioners' sugar. Beat until smooth, creamy, and right to spread. Add more cream if too thick.

Pineapple Upside-Down Cake

¼ cup margarine
½ cup brown sugar
3 eggs, beaten
1 cup sugar
½ cup pineapple juice
1 teaspoon vanilla
1½ cups flour
1 teaspoon baking powder
Pineapple slices
Cherries

Melt margarine and brown sugar in iron frying pan. Beat eggs until light. Add 1 cup sugar, ½ cup pineapple juice, and vanilla. Add flour and baking powder.

Place pineapple slices in brown sugar mixture. Pour batter over all. Bake for 25 to 30 minutes at 350°. Cherries can be placed inside pineapple slices before or after baking.

▲ ▲ ▲

For those who believe
No proof is necessary.
For those who doubt
No proof is possible.
   —*Song of Bernadette*

▼ ▼ ▼

Peanut Butter Cake

Large cake:
2¼ cups sifted cake flour
1½ cups sugar
3 teaspoons baking powder
1 teaspoon salt
⅓ cup soft shortening
⅓ cup peanut butter
1 cup milk
2 eggs (⅓ to ½ cup)

Small cake:
1½ cups
1 cup
2 teaspoons
½ teaspoon
½ cup
¼ cup
⅔ cup
1 egg (¼ cup)

Sift together flour, sugar, baking powder, and salt. Add soft shortening, peanut butter (not oily), and milk. Beat 2 minutes. Add eggs and beat 2 more minutes. Pour batter into 2 9-inch (large cake) or 2 8-inch (small cake) prepared pans. Bake 25 to 30 minutes.

Strawberry Whip Cake Topping

1 cup granulated sugar
1 egg white

½ to 1 cup strawberries

Place all ingredients in bowl and beat for several minutes or until stiff. Spread on sheet cake and top with whole berries.

60-Second Icing

1 cup semisweet chocolate pieces
¼ cup butter

½ cup canned milk
1½ cups confectioners' sugar

Melt chocolate and butter together; allow to cool; blend in sugar with milk. Beat briskly.

▲ ▲ ▲

Generosity consists not in the sum given, but in the manner in which it is bestowed.

▼ ▼ ▼

Mile High Icing

1 egg white
1 cup white syrup
1 teaspoon vanilla

Put in electric mixer bowl and beat for several minutes or until as stiff as you like it. It takes from 10 to 15 minutes to make it really pile up high.

Burnt Sugar Icing

2 cups white sugar
1 cup cream (don't use canned milk)
2 tablespoons white sugar
¼ cup butter
Pinch of salt

Put 2 cups sugar and cream in pan and let come to a boil. Burn 2 tablespoons white sugar in skillet or pan and stir, while pouring, into other mixture. Let come to a boil (245°). Add butter after removing from fire; pinch of salt.

▲ ▲ ▲

"Woman was taken out of man—Not out of his head, to rule over him; nor out of his feet, to be trampled under by him; but out of his side, to be equal to him—under his arm, that he might protect her, and near his heart that he might love her."

—*Matthew Henry*

▼ ▼ ▼

Candy

Foolproof Fudge

1 tall can evaporated milk
2 tablespoons butter or margarine
4½ cups sugar
Dash of salt

Combine above ingredients, bring to vigorous boil, stirring often. Reduce heat and continue to cook (simmer) about six minutes.

Put 2 cups (a 12-ounce package or 3 4-ounce bars) sweet cooking chocolate, broken in small pieces, and 1 pint marshmallow creme in large bowl. Gradually pour the boiling syrup over the chocolate-marshmallow mixture and beat until the chocolate melts. Stir in 1 to 2 cups of broken walnut meats. Pour into buttered pans.

Honey-Sugared Walnuts

2½ cups walnut halves
1½ cups sugar
½ cup water
¼ cup honey
½ teaspoon salt
½ teaspoon cinnamon
½ teaspoon vanilla

Toast walnuts in moderate oven (375°) for ten minutes, stirring once. Combine sugar, water, honey, salt, and cinnamon in pan and cook to soft-ball stage (236°). Remove from heat and beat until mixture begins to get creamy. Add vanilla and warm nuts; stir gently until nuts are well coated and mixture becomes thick. Turn out on buttered baking sheet and with two forks separate the nuts at once.

Peanut Butter Fudge

- 2 cups sugar
- 2/3 cup milk
- 1 cup marshmallow creme
- 1 cup chunk-style peanut butter
- 1 6-ounce package (1 cup) semisweet chocolate pieces
- 1 teaspoon vanilla

Combine sugar and milk. Heat and stir over medium heat until sugar dissolves and mixture comes to boiling. Cook to 234° (soft-ball stage). Remove from heat; add remaining ingredients and stir well. Pour into 9x9-inch buttered pan. Score in squares while warm; cut when firm.

Hawaiian Panocha

- 1 cup granulated sugar
- 1/2 cup brown sugar
- Dash salt
- 1/4 cup light cream
- 1/2 cup well-drained, crushed pineapple
- 1 tablespoon butter
- 1/2 teaspoon vanilla
- Walnut halves

Combine sugars, salt, cream, and pineapple. Stir to dissolve sugar. Heat to boiling. Cook to soft-ball stage (236°); stir occasionally. Remove from heat. Add butter or fortified margarine. Cool to lukewarm (110°) without stirring. Add vanilla. Beat until thick. Spread quickly into greased 6-inch square pan. Top with walnut halves.

▲ ▲ ▲

Kind hearts are the gardens;
Kind thoughts are the roots;
Kind words are the flowers;
Kind deeds are the fruits.
  —Anonymous

▼ ▼ ▼

Caramel Snappers

72 (about 1 cup) pecan halves
36 caramels
2 1-ounce squares candy-making chocolate, melted

Grease baking sheet; on it arrange pecans, flat side down, in groups of 4. Place 2 caramels on each cluster of pecans. Heat in slow oven (325°) till caramels soften, about 8 minutes. Remove from oven; with a buttered spatula, flatten caramels over pecans. Cool; remove from pan to waxed paper. Brush tops with melted chocolate. Makes 18.

Molasses Taffy

"Mild molasses, rich nut flavor. Fun to pull—"

½ cup brown sugar
1¼ cups light molasses
¾ cup light corn syrup
¼ teaspoon soda
1½ tablespoons butter
1 cup chopped nuts

Combine sugar, molasses, and syrup. Stir to dissolve sugar. Cook to light-crack stage (265°). Add soda and butter; mix well. Add nutmeats. Pour into greased shallow pan. When cool enough to handle, pull until *very* light. Form in ropes; cut with scissors.

▲ ▲ ▲

*"Twixt optimist and pessimist
The difference is droll;
The optimist sees the doughnut,
The pessimist, the hole."*
—McLandburgh Wilson

▼ ▼ ▼

Cookies

Soft Sugar Cookies

- 2 eggs
- 1½ cups sugar
- 1 cup shortening
- 1 cup milk (sweet)
- 1 teaspoon vanilla
- 4 cups flour
- 2 teaspoons baking powder
- 2 teaspoons cream of tartar
- 2 teaspoons soda (scant)

Beat eggs 1 minute. Add sugar and shortening and beat 1 minute. Add vanilla and milk. Sift dry ingredients and combine with first mixture. Drop by spoon onto cookie sheet and bake. When cool—ice.

Frosting

- 6 tablespoons butter (room temperature)
- ⅛ teaspoon salt
- 1 pound confectioners' sugar
- 2 teaspoons vanilla
- 4 to 5 tablespoons milk

Put all ingredients in bowl and beat at high speed 1 minute. Divide icing into several parts and color each with food coloring. Makes variety out of one batch of cookies.

Crescents

- 1½ cups shortening
- 1½ cups powdered sugar
- 4 cups flour
- 1 teaspoon salt
- 1 cup chopped pecans
- ⅔ cup evaporated milk, not diluted
- 3 teaspoons vanilla

Cream in mixer shortening and sugar. Gradually add flour and milk alternately. Stir in salt, nuts, and vanilla. Chill. Make ball, lengthen and make in shape of crescent. Bake 10 to 12 minutes at 350°. Dust with powdered sugar after somewhat cooled.

Ginger Cookies

⅔ cup shortening
1 cup sugar
¼ cup dark molasses
2 cups flour
1 teaspoon ginger

1 beaten egg
1 teaspoon salt
1 teaspoon baking soda
1 teaspoon cinnamon
1 teaspoon cloves

Thoroughly cream shortening and sugar. Add egg and molasses and beat well. Add sifted dry ingredients and mix thoroughly. Chill dough. Roll on floured board. Bake at 350° about 10 minutes on greased cookie sheet. Yield 4 dozen large cookies.

Drop Cookies

½ cup butter
1½ cups sugar
½ cup milk
3 cups quick oats

1 cup coconut
2 tablespoons cocoa
1 teaspoon vanilla

Bring butter, milk and sugar to boil. Cool awhile. Add quick oats, coconut, cocoa, vanilla. Mix and drop on waxed paper.

Caramel Squares

2 cups brown sugar
½ cup butter
2 cups flour
1 cup chopped pecans
2 whole eggs

2 level teaspoons baking powder
2 teaspoons vanilla
Pinch of salt

Melt butter and brown sugar; add eggs and beat well, then add baking powder mixed with flour, vanilla, nuts, and salt. Pour into large, shallow buttered pan. Bake 30 minutes at 300°. When cool, cut in squares.

Oatmeal Macaroons

1 cup shortening	1 teaspoon soda
1 cup brown sugar	½ teaspoon salt
1 cup white sugar	½ teaspoon cinnamon
½ teaspoon vanilla	3 cups uncooked oats
2 eggs, unbeaten	1 cup chopped nuts
1¼ cups flour	1 cup raisins

Place shortening, sugars, vanilla, and eggs in mixing bowl; beat thoroughly. Sift flour, soda, salt, spices. Add to shortening mixture, and mix again. Fold in oats, nuts, and raisins. Drop by spoonful onto greased baking sheet. Flatten if desired. Bake at 350° for 12 to 15 minutes. Cool 2 minutes and remove from baking sheet. Makes 5½ to 6 dozen.

Brown Edge Cookies

½ cup butter (¼ pound)	¾ cup flour
⅓ cup sugar	1 teaspoon vanilla
1 egg, well beaten	

Mix all ingredients and drop on buttered cookie sheet one inch apart. Bake slowly (325°). If desired, place nuts or raisins in center of each cookie.

Chocolate Macaroons

4 egg whites	½ teaspoon salt
¼ cup water	1 tablespoon flour
⅔ cup sugar	2 ounces chocolate, melted
2 teaspoons vanilla	2½ cups shredded coconut

Beat egg whites with cold water until stiff, but not dry. Beat in sugar and vanilla. Add salt and flour and blend carefully. Fold in melted chocolate and coconut. Drop from teaspoon onto heavy paper on baking sheet. Bake 25 to 30 minutes at 325°.

Chocolate Mint Cookies

3 cups flour
1 teaspoon soda
½ teaspoon salt

1 cup butter
1 cup sugar
½ cup brown sugar

. . .

2 eggs, unbeaten
1 tablespoon water
1 teaspoon vanilla

Chocolate mints
Nuts

Sift flour, soda, and salt together. Set aside. Cream butter or margarine, white sugar, and brown sugar, firmly packed. Add eggs, water, and vanilla. Beat well.

Blend dry ingredients in gradually. Mix thoroughly. Cover and chill for at least 2 hours.

Enclose a chocolate mint wafer in about 1 tablespoon of chilled dough. Place on greased baking sheet about 2 inches apart. Top each cookie with a walnut or pecan half. Bake in 375° oven for 10 to 12 minutes.

Burnt Butter Glaze

2 tablespoons butter
2 cups confectioners' sugar
¼ cup evaporated milk

Heat butter until golden brown. Beat in, until smooth, the sifted confectioners' sugar and the evaporated milk. Ices about 4 dozen cookies.

▲ ▲ ▲

"If our boys and girls are not so good as they were when you were a child their age, it may be that they had a much better mother and dad than your child has."

—*Anonymous*

▼ ▼ ▼

Jubilee Jumbles

- ½ cup shortening
- 2 eggs
- 1 cup brown sugar (packed)
- ½ cup white sugar
- 1 cup undiluted evaporated milk
- 1 teaspoon vanilla
- 2¾ cups sifted flour
- ½ teaspoon salt
- ½ teaspoon baking soda
- 1 cup shredded coconut or dates or nuts

Sift flour, soda, and salt. Blend in remaining ingredients. Drop by tablespoon two inches apart on greased baking sheet. Bake until a light touch with finger leaves no imprint (about 10 minutes). While cookies are still warm, frost, if desired, with Burnt Butter Glaze.

Thumbprint Cookies

- ½ cup soft shortening
- ¼ cup brown sugar
- 1 cup flour
- ¼ teaspoon salt
- 1 egg, separated
- ½ teaspoon vanilla
- ¾ cup finely chopped nuts
- Jelly or confectioners' sugar

Blend shortening, brown sugar, egg yolk, and vanilla. Sift the flour and salt, and stir into first mixture. Roll into 1-inch balls. Dip in slightly beaten egg whites. Roll in finely chopped nuts. Place about 1 inch apart on ungreased baking sheet. Bake 5 minutes at 375°. Remove from oven and quickly press thumb gently on top of each cookie. Return to oven and bake 8 minutes longer. Cool. Place sparkling jelly or tinted confectioners' sugar icing in thumbprints.

▲ ▲ ▲

"A friend is a present you give yourself"
—*Anonymous*

▼ ▼ ▼

Peanut Butter Cookies

½ cup shortening
½ cup granulated sugar
½ cup peanut butter
½ cup brown sugar
1 egg
1¼ cups flour
¾ teaspoon baking powder
¼ teaspoon soda

Cream together shortening, granulated sugar, peanut butter, and brown sugar. Add 1 well-beaten egg. Beat well. Sift dry ingredients, and add to the butter and egg mixture. Mix thoroughly; chill for ½ hour. Roll into a small ball shape about size of a walnut. Place on greased cookie sheet an inch apart. Flatten each ball with a fork, crisscrossing the cookie. Bake in moderate oven.

Unbaked Cookies

2 cups sugar
4 tablespoons cocoa
1 square oleo
½ cup milk
3 cups raw oatmeal
½ cup nutmeats
½ cup peanut butter
1 teaspoon vanilla

Combine sugar, cocoa, oleo, and milk. Cook until mixture has boiled for 1 minute. Stir in the raw oatmeal, peanut butter, nutmeats, and vanilla. Mix well and drop by spoonfuls on wax paper. No baking.

▲ ▲ ▲

Come in the evening, come in the morning
Come when expected, come without warning;
Thousands of welcomes, you'll find here before you,
And the oftener you come, the more we'll adore you.

—*Anonymous*

▼ ▼ ▼

Swedish Gem Cookies

3 eggs
2¼ cups sifted flour
1 teaspoon salt
⅛ teaspoon soda
½ cup butter or margarine
½ cup shortening
½ cup sugar
½ teaspoon vanilla
2 or 3 tablespoons colored sugar
2 tablespoons candied fruit or nut topping

Separate two egg yolks from whites. Drop yolks from saucer, one at a time, into hot, salted water. Simmer until hard-cooked. Put through wire sieve.

Sift together flour, salt, and soda. Cream butter or margarine and shortening. Add gradually ½ cup sugar, creaming well. Add 1 unbeaten egg, ½ teaspoon vanilla, and the sieved egg yolks. Beat well. Blend in the dry ingredients. Chill if necessary for easy handling.

Press through a cookie press onto ungreased baking sheets or chill dough at least 2 hours and roll out on well-floured pastry cloth or board to ⅛-inch thickness. Cut into desired shapes with floured cookie cutter or pastry wheel. Place on ungreased baking sheets. Sprinkle with colored sugar and the finely chopped candied fruit or nut topping. Each is sufficient for 3 dozen cookies. Bake in moderate oven for 8 to 12 minutes, 375°.

▲ ▲ ▲

"America's future will be determined by the home and the school. The child becomes largely what it is taught, hence we must watch what we teach it, and how we live before it."
—*Jane Addams*

▼ ▼ ▼

Lemon Nut Refrigerator Cookies

2 cups flour
¼ teaspoon baking soda
¼ teaspoon salt
1 cup shortening
½ cup brown sugar
½ cup granulated sugar
1 egg, beaten
2 tablespoons lemon juice
1 tablespoon grated lemon rind
½ cup nuts

Sift together flour, salt, and soda. Mix shortening and sugars; then add beaten egg, lemon juice, and rind. Add flour mixture with the nuts. Form into roll and chill. Bake about 10 minutes at 400°. Makes 4½ dozen.

Date and Nut Squares

½ cup shortening
1½ cups brown sugar
½ teaspoon salt
1¼ teaspoons vanilla
1 egg, unbeaten yolk
½ cup coconut
¾ cup sifted all-purpose flour
1 teaspoon baking powder
¾ cup chopped walnuts
½ cup chopped dates

Mix shortening, 1 cup brown sugar, salt, vanilla, and unbeaten egg yolk. Sift flour with baking powder—blend the mixture. Add coconut, ½ cup chopped walnuts, and dates. Spread batter in pan evenly. Beat egg white in peaks, beat in remaining sugar and vanilla. Spread on batter with remaining ground walnuts and bake 35 minutes in 325° oven. Cut in squares while hot.

▲ ▲ ▲

Try a dash of kindness with a pinch of love today. Top it off with a bit of cheerfulness and add a touch of goodwill. See how much better the day can be!

▼ ▼ ▼

Peanut Butter Brownies

2 eggs	1⅓ cups unsifted flour
1 cup granulated sugar	1 tablespoon baking powder
½ cup brown sugar	½ teaspoon salt
¼ cup peanut butter	2 tablespoons peanuts, chopped
2 tablespoons margarine	
1 teaspoon vanilla	

Combine eggs, sugars, peanut butter, margarine and vanilla. Beat at medium speed until thoroughly blended. Add flour, baking powder and salt and continue mixing until mixture is smooth. Spread batter in a greased 9-inch square pan and sprinkle with chopped peanuts. Bake in moderate oven (350°) for 30 minutes. Cut in squares while warm.

Baked Fudge

¼ cup milk	½ cup flour
2 ounces chocolate	1 teaspoon vanilla
⅓ cup shortening	2 eggs
. . .	½ teaspoon salt
1 cup sugar	1 cup nutmeats

Heat milk and melt chocolate and shortening in it. Mix in a bowl the remaining ingredients. Combine contents of pan and bowl. Spread on greased 12x16-inch pan. Bake 10 minutes in 325° oven. Remove from oven and spread on chocolate icing. Cut in squares when cold.

Icing: Mix together 1½ tablespoons melted butter, 1¼ cups confectioners' sugar, 1 teaspoon vanilla, and 2 squares chocolate (melted). If necessary, add evaporated milk for easier spreading.

▲ ▲ ▲

The soul is dyed the color of its leisure thoughts.

▼ ▼ ▼

Fudge Brownies

- ½ cup flour
- ½ teaspoon salt
- ⅓ cup shortening
- 1 cup sugar
- 1 cup walnuts
- ½ teaspoon baking powder
- 3 squares unsweetened chocolate
- 2 eggs
- 1 teaspoon vanilla

Melt chocolate and shortening in top of double boiler over boiling water. Remove from water. Beat eggs well, add sugar and vanilla. Mix thoroughly. Stir into melted chocolate and shortening. Add sifted dry ingredients and blend well. Add walnuts; stir just enough to mix. Spread mixture in greased pan, 8x8x2 inches. Bake at 350° for 30 to 35 minutes. Place pan on rack to cool. Cut when thoroughly cool.

Date Sugar Drops

- 1½ cups fresh dates
- 1 cup soft shortening (part butter)
- 1 cup brown sugar (packed)
- ¼ teaspoon maple flavoring
- 1 large egg
- 2 cups sifted flour
- 1 teaspoon baking powder
- ½ teaspoon baking soda
- ½ teaspoon salt

Pit dates, cut into small pieces. Beat together shortening, sugar, flavoring and egg until fluffy. Stir in dates. Sift together remaining ingredients and add to creamed mixture. Drop by small spoonfuls, about two inches apart, onto an ungreased cookie sheet. Bake in moderate (350°) oven until a light golden brown. Cool thoroughly before storing.

▲ ▲ ▲

"Keep your face to the sunshine and you cannot see the shadows."

—*Helen Keller*

▼ ▼ ▼

Date Pinwheel Cookies

Filling:
1 cup nuts	1 pound dates
½ cup sugar	½ cup water

Use coarse grinder for nuts and dates. Cook all of the above ingredients slowly. Stir, put lid on and let steam for a while. Cool before using.

1 cup shortening	1 teaspoon baking powder
1 cup white sugar	1 teaspoon soda
1 cup brown sugar	1 teaspoon cinnamon
3 eggs	¼ teaspoon salt
4 cups flour	1 teaspoon vanilla

Cream shortening and sugars. Add eggs and mix well. Beat until creamy. Sift dry ingredients, add to mixture. Add vanilla. Roll ¼ inch thick and spread with filling. Roll like jelly roll and put in refrigerator overnight. Slice. Bake 10 minutes at 350°.

Pecan Crisps

1½ cups sifted flour	3 tablespoons milk
1 cup sugar	1 teaspoon vanilla
¾ teaspoon salt	1 cup pecans, finely chopped
½ cup soft shortening	
1 egg, separated	

Heat oven to 375°. Sift flour, sugar, salt into bowl. Mix in thoroughly with fork: shortening, egg yolk, milk, vanilla. Form into balls size of small walnut. Place on ungreased baking pan. Press to 1/16-inch thickness using bottom of greased glass dipped in sugar. Brush with slightly beaten egg white. Sprinkle with pecans. Bake 8 to 10 minutes. Do not overbake. Makes about 5 dozen.

Ice Box Cookies

2 cups brown sugar	2 eggs
1 cup melted butter or margarine (½ pound)	3½ cups sifted flour
	1 cup black walnuts

Cream sugar, butter, and eggs. Add nuts, and stir in flour. Make several rolls. Put in ice box 10 hours. Slice and bake in moderate oven.

Breakfast Dunking Cookies (Pennsylvania Dutch)

2 eggs	1 cup brown sugar
1 cup white sugar (scant)	½ cup butter
1 cup sour cream	1 teaspoon soda
1 teaspoon baking powder	1 tsp. vanilla

Mix all ingredients. Roll dough out on floured pastry cloth, cut cookies and bake 8 to 10 minutes in moderate oven (350°).

Bon Bon Cookies

1 cup butter	2½ cups sifted flour
1 egg, well beaten	1 teaspoon baking powder
1 cup confectioners' sugar	

Blend well butter, egg, and sugar. Sift dry ingredients; add to first mixture and blend well. Wrap in waxed paper. Chill 1 hour. Form into small balls and place on cookie sheet. Flatten slightly and put nut kernel on top of each, if desired. Brush surface with a little milk. Sprinkle with granulated sugar. Bake at 375° for 12 to 15 minutes. Makes 4 dozen cookies.

▲ ▲ ▲

"It takes less time to do a thing right than it does to explain why you did it wrong."
—Henry Wadsworth Longfellow

▼ ▼ ▼

Date Bars

½ pound chopped dates
¾ cup water
½ cup sugar
1⅓ cups raw oatmeal
1⅓ cups flour
1 teaspoon soda
1 cup light brown sugar
¾ cup shortening or butter

Cook over low heat the chopped dates, water, and ½ cup sugar. Stir constantly.

Mix together raw oatmeal, flour, and soda. In another bowl combine light brown sugar and shortening or butter. Then combine oatmeal and brown sugar mixtures. Spread layer of dry mixture in 13x9x2-inch baking pan. Add date mixture and top with remaining dry mixture. Bake at 350° for 25 to 30 minutes.

Dream Bars

½ cup butter
½ cup brown sugar
1 cup flour
. . .
2 eggs, well beaten
1 cup brown sugar
1 teaspoon vanilla
2 tablespoons flour
1 teaspoon baking powder
½ teaspoon salt
1 cup shredded coconut
1 cup nutmeats

Blend butter, brown sugar, and flour and press mixture firmly in shallow 8x10-inch pan. Bake for 15 minutes at 350°.

Mix eggs, sugar, and vanilla. Mix with flour, baking powder, and salt. Stir in coconut and nuts. Spread over baked mixture, return to oven and bake for 25 minutes. Cool and cut in bars.

▲ ▲ ▲

Thankfulness is more than words. It is an attitude toward life. Learn to say "thank you" for the little things as well as the great.

▼ ▼ ▼

Butter Cookies

5 cups flour
4 eggs
1 pound butter
2 cups sugar
1½ teaspoons baking powder
⅛ teaspoon salt
2 teaspoons vanilla

Cream eggs, butter, and sugar. Add sifted dry ingredients and vanilla. Chill until dough is hard. Roll thin, cut with favorite cookie cutter and bake 8 to 10 minutes in 350° oven. There is no water or milk in these butter cookies.

Butter Balls

1 cup sugar
3 egg yolks
3 cups sifted flour
Cream
¾ pound butter or margarine
1 teaspoon vanilla
¼ teaspoon baking powder
Currant jelly

Cream sugar and butter. Add egg yolks. Add flour, baking powder, and vanilla. If dough is too stiff, add a little cream. Shape into balls the size of small nut, place a small dent in center and fill with currant jelly. Bake on ungreased cookie sheet at 375° for 10 minutes.

Christmas Fruit Cookies

½ cup shortening
1 egg
1¾ cups flour
½ teaspoon soda
½ teaspoon nutmeg
½ cup chopped nuts
1 cup brown sugar
¼ cup cold coffee
1 cup raisins or chopped dates
½ teaspoon salt
½ teaspoon cinnamon

Cream shortening, sugar, and egg. Sift dry ingredients and add to creamed mixture alternately with coffee. Blend in nuts and fruit. Drop on greased cookie sheet. Bake for 8 to 10 minutes at 375°.

Pineapple Oatmeal Cookies

¼ cup granulated sugar	1 teaspoon salt
1 tablespoon cornstarch	1 cup brown sugar
1 cup crushed pineapple	2½ cups uncooked
1 teaspoon lemon juice	oatmeal
1 cup flour	1 cup shortening

Combine sugar and cornstarch. Add pineapple (do not drain) and cook slowly until thick and clear. Add lemon juice. Cool.

Sift together flour and salt. Mix flour, brown sugar, and oatmeal. Cut in shortening. Place half of this mixture in a greased 6x11-inch baking pan. Pat down. Spread with cooled pineapple mixture. Sprinkle remaining crumbs over top, patting smooth. Bake at 350° for 45 minutes. Cut into bars when cool.

Crescents

1½ cups shortening	1 cup chopped pecans
1½ cups powdered sugar	⅔ cup undiluted
4 cups flour	evaporated milk
1 teaspoon salt	3 teaspoons vanilla

Cream in mixer the shortening and sugar. Gradually add flour and milk alternately. Add salt and pecans. Chill. Form into balls, lengthen, and make in the shape of a crescent. Bake 10 to 12 minutes at 350°. Cool slightly and dust with powdered sugar.

"He is an eloquent man who can treat humble subjects with delicacy, lofty things impressively, and moderate things temperately."
—*Cicero*

Desserts

Ribbon Ice Box Cake

1 package cherry gelatin
Graham crackers
. . .
½ cup powdered sugar
1 egg yolk, unbeaten
¼ cup walnut meats
¼ cup butter
½ cup crushed pineapple (drained)
1 egg white, stiffly beaten

Prepare and cool gelatin. Mix powdered sugar, egg yolk, nutmeats, butter, and pineapple. Fold in stiffly beaten egg whites. Place a layer of graham crackers in loaf pan. Alternate layers of filling and crackers, until there are 3 of crackers and 2 of filling. When the gelatin has begun to stiffen, pour ½ on cake. Whip the rest and pour on top.

Cherry Crisp

¼ cup flour
¾ cup cherry juice
¼ teaspoon red coloring
1 cup sugar
Salt
1 can cherries
. . .
1½ cups flour
½ teaspoon baking soda
¼ teaspoon salt
. . .
¾ cup raw quick oats
1 cup brown sugar
½ cup shortening

Cook ½ cup flour, cherry juice, red coloring, sugar, salt, and cherries. Make crumb mix by sifting 1½ cups flour, baking soda, salt. Add to raw quick oats, brown sugar, and shortening, making crumbs. Put half of crumb mix into baking dish, add cherries, then remainder of crumb mix. Bake at 350° for 25 to 30 minutes in a 12x8x2-inch or 13x9x2-inch pan.

Apple Fritters

- 1 egg, separated
- 1/3 cup milk
- 1/2 cup flour
- 2 teaspoons sugar
- 1/4 teaspoon salt
- 1/2 teaspoon baking powder
- . . .
- 2 teaspoons cooking oil
- 2 tart apples
- Powdered sugar

Beat egg yolk until light. Combine with milk. Mix flour with sugar, salt, and baking powder. Sift twice and stir into egg and milk. Beat until smooth. Stir in 2 teaspoons cooking oil. Fold in stiffly beaten egg white. Cover. Let stand 30 minutes. Peel, quarter, and slice thin 2 tart apples. Stir into mixture and drop from spoon into hot fat. Drain on soft paper. Serve hot with powdered sugar.

Date Roll

- 1/2 pound chopped dates
- 1/2 pound marshmallows, cut finely
- 1/2 cup thin cream
- 1/2 cup nut meats
- 1/2 pound graham crackers (rolled)

Mix all ingredients together and form a roll and chill. Slice and serve with whipped cream.

Pear Dumplings

- Pears
- 2 cups flour
- 1 tablespoon shortening
- 1/2 tsp. salt
- 2/3 cup milk
- . . .
- 2 tbsp. flour
- 2 tbsp. butter

Pare as many pears as you wish. Boil until soft; sweeten with sugar to taste.

Dumplings: Blend flour and shortening. Rub together with a little salt, add milk to make a stiff dough. Roll into balls. Add to pears. Boil until soft. Brown flour in butter; add to pears and dumplings. Boil until thick. Serve hot.

Cream Puffs

¼ cup shortening
½ cup boiling water
½ cup sifted enriched flour
¼ teaspoon salt
2 eggs

Combine shortening and boiling water. Stir over low heat until shortening is melted. Add flour and salt all at once and beat until ingredients are completely smooth. Remove from heat. Add eggs, one at a time, beating vigorously after each addition. Drop from tablespoon to baking sheet, slightly greased. Leave 2 inches between puffs to permit spreading.

Bake 10 minutes in hot oven (450°). Lower temperature to 350° and continue baking 20 minutes longer. Puffs should be golden brown and crisp. When cold, cut off tops with a sharp knife. Fill with flavored whipped cream, ice cream, or a filling made from a pudding mix. Replace tops. Makes 8 large cream puffs.

Best-Ever Pudding

1 cup brown sugar
2 cups water
Lump of butter
. . .
1 tablespoon butter
½ cup milk
½ cup white sugar
1 cup flour
½ cup raisins
1 teaspoon cinnamon
1 teaspoon nutmeg
2 teaspoons baking powder

Mix brown sugar, water, and lump of butter the size of a walnut. Bring these ingredients to a boil.

Mix all other ingredients thoroughly. Drop this batter into brown sugar syrup and bake 15 minutes in a moderate oven (350°). Can be served plain or with whipped cream.

Orange Charlotte (low in calories)

1 package orange gelatin
1 6-ounce can frozen orange juice
3 tablespoons fresh or frozen lemon juice
¼ cup sugar
⅓ cup ice water
⅓ cup nonfat dry milk
1 dozen lady fingers or sponge cake
1 cup hot water
1 teaspoon grated lemon rind, if desired

Dissolve gelatin in the boiling water, add unthawed orange juice and lemon juice, sugar, and grated lemon rind. Let stand until the mixture thickens, not too stiff. Place ice water in small mixer bowl; add nonfat dry milk, beat until it stands in stiff peaks; add gelatin mixture and beat until fluffy. If mixture looks too thin, cool in refrigerator for 15 minutes. Arrange split lady fingers or sponge cake vertically around 8-inch springform pan, oblong dish or sherbet glasses. Pour in slightly thickened orange mixture.

Black Cherry Mold

1 package black cherry Jello
1 cup hot water
1 can pitted black cherries
. . .
Cream cheese
Milk

Dissolve black cherry Jello in hot water. Add pitted black cherries. Refrigerate.

Thin the cream cheese with milk, and use as topping.

▲ ▲ ▲

Besides red and yellow there are other colors in the rainbow. The somber blue and purple give richer meaning to the gay colors. Life's sorrows can help us to have an appreciation for its brighter days.

▼ ▼ ▼

DESSERTS

Ice Cream

1⅔ cups evaporated milk
⅔ cup sugar
1 envelope instant soft drink mix

Chill evaporated milk (1 tall can) in an ice tray until it is almost frozen at the edges. Put the ice-cold milk into 1½-quart size bowl. Whip at high speed until fluffy. Add sugar and 1 envelope instant soft drink mix and whip until stiff. Freeze in a 1-quart ice tray until firm, 3 to 4 hours.

Layered Fruit Fluff

Melt ½ pound (32 to 34) marshmallows (or 4 cups miniature marshmallows) with 1 cup milk in top of double boiler over boiling water. Chill until completely cold and slightly thickened.

Combine 1¼ cups flour, ½ cup firmly packed brown sugar, ¼ teaspoon salt.

Cut in ½ cup butter or margarine until particles are fine. Place mixture in a 12x8 or 13x9-inch pan.

Bake at 400° for 10 to 12 minutes, stirring occasionally, until golden brown. Cool. Remove ½ cup of mixture; press remainder into bottom of pan.

Beat 1 cup whipping cream, ¼ teaspoon almond extract until thick.

Fold cooled marshmallow mixture into whipped cream. Turn ⅔ of mixture into pan; spread to cover crumb layer.

Spoon 1 can (1 pound 6 ounce) cherry, blueberry or other fruit pie filling over marshmallow layer; top with remaining marshmallow mixture. Sprinkle reserved crumbs over top. Chill at least 6 hours or overnight before serving. Serves 12.
(If desired, cooled lemon pie filling may be substituted. Use a pie filling or your favorite recipe.)

Date Pudding

½-pound package dates, cut fine	1 tablespoon melted butter
1 teaspoon soda	1 cup nutmeats, chopped fine
1 cup hot water	1 cup flour
1 cup sugar	1 teaspoon salt
1 egg beaten	1 teaspoon vanilla

Dissolve soda in hot water; pour this over finely cut dates. Cool. Mix remainder of ingredients in order as listed. Fold in first mixture, and bake 1 hour at 250°.

Floating Island

1 large can evaporated milk	½ cup sugar
4 eggs	2 tablespoons cornstarch (dissolved in water)
1 tablespoon vanilla	

Separate eggs. Scald milk and pour into bowl in which sugar and egg yolks have been blended. Return this mixture to heat, and stir in cornstarch. Bring to a boil while stirring. Add vanilla.

Pour into baking dish and top with meringue which is made from egg whites. Bake until brown in 350° oven.

▲ ▲ ▲

"I decided that I would make my life my argument. I would advocate the things I believed in terms of the life I lived and what I did."

—*Albert Schweitzer*

▼ ▼ ▼

Cherry Nut Creme

- 1 package vanilla pudding (¾ ounce)
- 1¾ cups milk
- 1 tablespoon unflavored gelatine
- ¼ cup milk
- 1 cup heavy cream
- ½ teaspoon vanilla
- ¼ cup sugar
- 16 vanilla wafers
- ½ cup diced marshmallows
- ½ cup chopped walnuts
- ½ cup chopped maraschino cherries

Prepare pudding as directed on package, using 1¾ cups milk. Soften gelatin in ¼ cup milk. Stir into hot pudding until gelatin dissolves. Cool at room temperature.

Whip cream and add sugar and vanilla. Fold into pudding.

Line an 8-inch square baking dish with vanilla wafers. Pour over wafers one half of pudding mixture; sprinkle with marshmallows and half of chopped nuts and cherries. Pour over remaining pudding and top with remaining walnuts and cherries. Chill thoroughly. Cut in squares and serve with whipped cream. Serves 9.

Apple Nut Pudding

- ¾ cup sugar
- 1 well-beaten egg
- ½ cup flour
- ½ teaspoon salt
- 1 teaspoon baking powder
- 1 cup chopped tart apples
- ½ cup walnuts
- 1 teaspoon almond extract

Combine all ingredients and bake in 8-inch square pan in 350° oven for 35 minutes.

▲ ▲ ▲

"When we worry we are playing God;
When we have concern we are used by God."
—Roy Burkhart

▼ ▼ ▼

Collins Dessert

¾ cup butter or margarine	1 cup nutmeats
1 cup sugar	Graham crackers, crushed
3 eggs, separated	. . .
1 small can crushed pineapple	2 packages red gelatin
1 tablespoon cornstarch	Whipped cream

Combine and cook: butter, sugar, *egg yolks,* pineapple, and cornstarch. Cool, then add nutmeats, coarsely chopped. Beat egg whites until very stiff and fold into cooled pineapple mixture.

Line a 9x15-inch baking dish with crushed graham crackers. Add filling and cover with top layer of graham cracker crumbs.

Prepare red gelatin, and chill until slightly thickened. Pour over top of pudding mixture and chill for about 24 hours. Cover with a thin layer of whipped cream just before serving.

▲ ▲ ▲

Don't give me of tomorrow!
Give me the man who'll say
That when a good deed's to be done,
"Let's do the deed today."
—Anonymous

▼ ▼ ▼

Meat Dishes

Chow Mein Hot Dish

1 to 1½ pounds hamburger	2 cans water
1 large onion, diced	½ cup uncooked rice
1 can chicken-rice soup	1 cup celery, diced
1 can mushroom soup	3 tablespoons soy sauce
	1 small can mushrooms

Brown hamburger and diced onion. Mix with remaining ingredients and bake 1 hour at 350°.
Last 15 minutes: sprinkle Chinese noodles on top.

Chicken and Biscuit Pie

1 1-pound can of chicken in gravy	1 small diced onion
1 can condensed cream of chicken soup	1 8-ounce can of peas
1 tablespoon instant onion or	1 3-ounce can of mushrooms
	1 package refrigerated biscuits

Mix chicken in gravy, soup, and seasonings. Add drained peas and mushrooms. Heat slowly, stirring now and then, until bubbling hot; turn into a 1½-quart casserole. Arrange the biscuits on top of the casserole and bake in a hot oven (425°) for about 15 minutes, or until biscuits are done.

▲ ▲ ▲

The greatest happiness of life is the conviction that we are loved—loved for ourselves, or rather, loved in spite of ourselves.
—*Victor Hugo*

▼ ▼ ▼

Stuffed Peppers

14 medium-sized peppers	3 medium onions, minced
1½ pounds lean hamburger	1 cup rice (before cooking)
2 or 3 tablespoons or ½ stick butter	1 No. 303 can tomatoes
	Salt and pepper to taste

Boil rice until almost tender. Wash all the starch out so it won't be sticky.

Brown meat in skillet. Add the onions, saute 5 minutes, pour in rice, tomatoes, salt and pepper. Cook about 2 minutes.

Wash peppers and cut tops off carefully; save tops for covers. Stuff peppers and replace the tops. Arrange in baking pan. Add 1½ cups water and bake 1 hour. Baste peppers occasionally with pan juice. Serve hot. This will serve 7, allowing 2 peppers each, with green salad and dessert.

Sour Beef and Potato Dumplings

3 pounds beef cubed	1 teaspoon mixed whole spices (including bay leaf)
1½ cups vinegar	
2 cups water	
1 large onion	1 teaspoon salt
	⅛ teaspoon pepper

Combine the above ingredients in a large bowl and set in refrigerator overnight. Remove meat and brown in 1 tablespoon hot fat. Return to the other ingredients and simmer for 2 to 2½ hours, or until tender.

Fifteen minutes before serving, soften 10 or 12 ginger snaps in a cup water. Add to liquid and boil to make gravy. Serve over potato dumplings.

Potato Dumplings

5 or 6 potatoes (medium size)
1½ teaspoons salt
1 teaspoon baking powder
1 cup flour
1 egg, slightly beaten
2 slices bread cut in cubes
2 tablespoons butter

Cook potatoes in skins. Cool and mash, adding salt, egg, baking powder, and flour. Add more flour if needed to make a stiff dough. Fry bread cubes in butter until golden. Mix into dough or roll dough around cubes, making balls about 2 inches in diameter. Boil 12 minutes in about 2 quarts of water in a large kettle.

Company Chicken Ring

¼ cup butter or margarine
½ cup flour
1 teaspoon salt
3 cups chicken stock
½ cup milk
1 teaspoon lemon juice
Pepper to taste
Paprika
3 cups diced, cooked chicken
½ cup sliced stuffed olives
2 tablespoons chopped pimiento
½ teaspoon poultry seasoning

Melt butter and stir in flour. Add salt, stock, and milk. Cook over low heat till thick, stirring constantly. Add remaining ingredients. Heat. Serve in center of biscuit ring.

Biscuit rings: Sift together 1½ cups flour, 3 teaspoons baking powder, ¾ teaspoon salt, and ½ teaspoon poultry seasoning. Cut in ¼ cup shortening. Stir in ½ cup plus 2 tablespoons milk. Bake in greased 8-inch ring mold in hot oven (450°) for 15 minutes. Turn onto hot serving plate. Brush with butter and fill with hot chicken. Serves six.

Ground Beef and Tomato
(topped with corn bread mix)

2 tablespoons oil
¼ cup chopped onions
1 can tomato sauce
2 tablespoons catsup
Salt and pepper
1 pound ground beef
½ package corn bread mix

Fry beef and onion in oil. Mix sauce and catsup, pour in casserole, top with corn bread mixture. Bake in 400° oven for 20 minutes.

Buttermilk Fried Chicken

1 frying chicken, cut up
1 small onion, cut up
Salt and pepper to taste
1 cup or more buttermilk
Shortening and flour

Salt and pepper chicken, dip in buttermilk, then in flour. Dip in buttermilk again, then in flour again. Fry in very hot fat until brown. Remove chicken from fat. Brown flour for gravy. Add onion and simmer about 1 minute. Add ½ to ¾ cup of buttermilk and enough water to make the gravy as thick as you like it. Put chicken back into gravy and pressure cook for 5 minutes. Let cool normally, and remove chicken from gravy and serve.

▲ ▲ ▲

There is not the least flower but seems to hold up its head and to look pleasantly, in the secret sense of the goodness of its heavenly Maker.

▼ ▼ ▼

Tuna Macaroni Casserole

2 cups cooked macaroni	1 7-ounce can of tuna
. . .	¼ cup minced onion
1 can cream of mushroom soup	½ cup shredded cheese
½ cup milk	. . .
	Grated cheese

Mix cream of mushroom soup with milk. Add tuna (drained and flaked), minced onion, and shredded cheese. Add this to the drained, cooked macaroni. Sprinkle some grated cheese on top. (Refrigerate if you care to, but remove ½ hour before putting it in the oven.) Bake about ½ hour or a little longer at 350°.

Tomato Burgers

1 tablespoon shortening	1 teaspoon chili powder
1 pound ground beef	Salt and pepper
½ cup chopped onion	1 can tomato soup
½ cup chopped celery	

In skillet, melt shortening; add ground beef, chopped onion, chopped celery, chili powder, and salt and pepper. Cook until meat is browned; stir to separate meat particles. Add 1 can tomato soup; simmer a few minutes. Serve on buns.

▲ ▲ ▲

If you are planning for one year, sow grain; ten years, plant trees; but when planning for one hundred years, grow men.
—Chinese proverb

▼ ▼ ▼

Grandmother's Scrapple

3 cups meat broth
4 cups boiled meat, cubed
Salt and pepper
Dash of cayenne

1½ teaspoons rubbed sage
. . .
1 cup yellow cornmeal

This is a delicious way to use leftover meat and broth. To broth in which meat has been boiled, add 4 cups boiled meat, cut into small cubes. Add salt to taste and a dash of pepper and cayenne, and rubbed sage. Heat to boiling. Sift in yellow cornmeal, stirring constantly. Cook for one half hour and pour into mold or loaf pan. Chill thoroughly. Slice and fry. This will keep very well in cool place, frying as it is needed.

Corned Beef Patties

2 tablespoons butter, melted
Chopped onion
2 tablespoons flour
1 can tomatoes (2 cups)
Pepper

1 can corned beef
2 cups flour
1 teaspoon baking soda
½ teaspoon salt
. . .
½ cup shortening

Stir together all ingredients except 2 cups flour, baking soda, salt, and shortening. Cook these slowly. In the meantime, sift together these remaining dry ingredients. Cut in ½ cup shortening. Add water to hold together. Roll out and cut into 8 squares and place in muffin tins. Fill with the cooked filling and fold dough over. Bake in 425° oven for 20 minutes.

▲ ▲ ▲

"One today is worth two tomorrows;
What I am to be I am now becoming."
—*Benjamin Franklin*

▼ ▼ ▼

MEAT DISHES

Chicken a la Can Can

- 1 can (10½ ounces) condensed cream of chicken soup
- 1 can (10½ ounces) condensed cream of celery soup
- 1 soup can of water
- ½ cup celery
- 1 can (12 ounces) boned chicken or 1½ cups boned cooked chicken pieces
- 1⅓ cups instant rice
- 1 can (3½ ounces) French fried onions

Combine the soups, water, celery, and chicken. Add instant rice, right from the box. Stir to mix. Bring quickly to a boil. Cover and reduce heat. Simmer about 7 minutes. Put in casserole, top with onions and put in slow oven for 15 to 20 minutes until onions are heated. Serves six.

Swedish Meatballs

- 1 pound ground beef
- ½ pound ground pork
- ½ cup minced onion
- ¾ cup fine dry bread crumbs
- 1 tablespoon minced parsley
- 1½ teaspoons salt
- ⅛ teaspoon pepper
- 1 teaspoon Worcestershire sauce
- 1 egg
- ½ cup milk

Thoroughly mix the above ingredients. Shape mixture into balls the size of a walnut. Brown in ¼ cup hot fat. Remove from heat and stir into the fat:

- ¼ cup flour
- 1 teaspoon paprika
- ⅛ teaspoon pepper
- ½ teaspoon salt

Stir in 2 cups boiling water and ¾ cup sour cream. Return meat to gravy and cook for 15 to 20 minutes. Makes 6 to 8 servings.

Meat 'n' Pepper Corn Bread

1 tablespoon shortening	½ teaspoon chili powder
½ cup chopped onion	1 teaspoon salt
1 pound ground beef	¼ teaspoon pepper
1 8-ounce can tomato sauce	1 recipe corn bread
	7 or 8 pepper rings

Lightly brown beef and onion in skillet, using shortening. Add tomato sauce and seasonings and simmer while preparing corn bread. Arrange the green pepper rings in a design in the bottom of a heavy skillet. Pour the meat mixture over the pepper rings, and then put the corn bread (made without sugar) on top. Bake 20 to 25 minutes at 425°.

Instant Tacos

1 pound ground beef	1 package Fritos
1 can chili without beans	

Brown meat lightly in skillet. Add chili and simmer until thoroughly blended. Place handful of Fritos in cereal bowl and cover with meat mixture. Serve piping hot!

Hot Tamale Pie

1 pound ground beef	1 can tomato sauce
1 onion, chopped	Can water
1 small green pepper, chopped	1 cup whole kernel corn
	2 teaspoons chili powder
Salt to taste	Corn bread

Fry meat, onion, pepper, and salt—don't brown. When this mixture has cooked a while, add 1 can tomato sauce, fill can with water and add, also. Then add whole kernel corn and chili powder. Simmer a little while. Make thin corn bread and spoon on top; bake in preheated oven until corn bread is done.

Meat Pinwheel Casserole

2 tablespoons fat or meat drippings
1½ cups ground, cooked meat
1 large onion, chopped
¼ teaspoon thyme
1½ teaspoons salt
¼ teaspoon pepper
1 No. 2 can peas
1 No. 2 can tomatoes
1½ tablespoons flour
Biscuit dough (made with 2 cups flour)

Heat fat in large skillet. Add meat, onion, and seasonings; brown lightly. Reserve 1 cup of the mixture for biscuit topping. To the remainder, add peas and tomatoes. Blend flour and a little water; add to meat and vegetables; cook until slightly thickened. Pour into 2-quart casserole. Roll biscuit dough into ¼-inch-thick rectangle. Spread with reserved meat mixture. Roll, jellyroll fashion, into long roll. Form in ring on top of mixture in casserole; press ends together. With scissors, cut slices through ring almost to center, about 1 inch apart. Turn each slice slightly on its side. Bake 20 to 25 minutes in very hot oven, 450°.

Italian Spaghetti

1 pound ground beef
1 can tomato soup
1 can Italian tomato paste
1 cup water
1 large onion, chopped
1 green pepper, chopped
½ teaspoon black pepper
1 lb. spaghetti
1 teaspoon salt
1 teaspoon sugar
½ teaspoon garlic salt
2 teaspoons chili powder
2 tablespoons Worcestershire sauce
2 tablespoons Italian grated cheese

Saute onion, pepper, and ground beef. Add tomato soup, paste, and other ingredients. Let cook slowly for two hours or more. All ingredients can be added more or less according to taste. Pour over hot cooked spaghetti. Serves from four to six.

Southern Style Beef Hash

½ cup diced green pepper
½ cup diced white onions
¼ cup diced celery
2 tablespoons butter or oleo
1 cup diced uncooked potatoes
2 cups cold finely diced roast beef
1 cup beef stock
Salt and pepper
2 tablespoons minced parsley, optional
1 tin of tomatoes or sauce, if desired

Saute pepper and onions over low heat in covered skillet 10 minutes; add all other ingredients except parsley. Cook slowly 40 minutes. Add water as needed. When potatoes are tender, fold in parsley. This can be served on chow mein noodles.

Sauteed Round Steak

Round steak
Seasoned flour
Hot butter or drippings

Cut a round steak ⅓-inch thick into 2x4-inch pieces. Dip into seasoned flour. Saute them until brown over a quick fire in hot butter or drippings. Reduce the heat to a very low flame, cover the pan and cook the steak until tender. Add water as needed.

Pork Roast in Applesauce Blanket

Pork roast
1½ cups thick applesauce
2 teaspoons horseradish
Brown sugar

Roast pork until almost done; ½ hour before it is finished, mix horseradish with applesauce and spread blanket of applesauce over roast. Sprinkle with small amount brown sugar. A slight crust will be formed on outside when meat is done.

Lazy Day Pot Roast

3 to 4 pounds beef chuck
¼ cup flour
¼ cup shortening
1 teaspoon salt
½ teaspoon pepper
⅓ cup horseradish
2 cups water
6 small peeled onions
6 washed carrots
6 pieces trimmed celery
3 peeled potatoes, cut in halves

Roll beef in flour, salt, and pepper. Brown on all sides in hot shortening. Spread beef with horseradish. Add water. Cover and cook over a low flame for 2 to 2½ hours. Add vegetables. Cook over a low flame for 1 hour.

Barbecued Pot Roast

1 3-pound beef pot roast
2 teaspoons salt
¼ teaspoon pepper
3 tablespoons fat
½ cup water
1 can tomato sauce
3 medium sliced onions
½ teaspoon garlic salt
2 tablespoons brown sugar
½ teaspoon dry mustard
¼ cup lemon juice
¼ cup catsup
¼ cup vinegar
1 tablespoon Worcestershire sauce

Rub meat with salt and pepper and brown in hot fat. Add water, tomato sauce, sliced onions, and garlic salt. Cover and simmer 1½ hours. Combine remaining ingredients and pour over meat; cover and continue cooking one hour. (Sauce also goes well with spare ribs.)

Ham Loaf

2 pounds ground ham
1 pound ground pork
2 eggs
1 can crushed pineapple
1 box corn flakes

Mix above ingredients all together in form of a loaf. Bake in oven 1 hour at 350°, with water in bottom of pan to keep from burning. Eight servings.

Noodle-Doodle

1 pound ground beef
1 can cream of mushroom soup
1 small onion
1 pound package of egg noodles
Salt and pepper

Roll ground beef into small balls and brown. Add onion, chopped fine, and simmer for a few minutes. In casserole, place layer of noodles, layer of ground beef, then noodles, and so on, leaving at least one inch from top. Add cream of mushroom soup and enough water to cover. Place in 350° oven and bake until noodles are tender. Serve.

Spanish Pork Chops with Rice

1 cup rice
6 pork chops
½ cup diced onion
½ cup diced celery
2 cups cooked tomatoes
1 teaspoon salt
½ teaspoon pepper
3 tablespoons minced parsley

Cook rice; brown pork chops and remove them from skillet. Add onion and celery to drippings in skillet and cook. Arrange chops in a baking dish, and top each one with a mound of rice. Add tomatoes, seasoning, and parsley to skillet. Stir together; then pour into baking dish. Cover and bake in oven at 350° for 1 hour. Serves 6.

Barbecued Spareribs

Place in bottom of heavy kettle a layer of small meaty spareribs. Cover with layer of sliced onions. Pour barbecue sauce over. Repeat layers. Cover. Bake at 325° until meat is tender (about 2 to 2½ hours). Uncover last half hour. Serve piping hot.

Barbecue Sauce

½ cup catsup
1½ teaspoons salt
⅛ teaspoon chili powder
1 cup water
1 tablespoon brown sugar
½ teaspoon mustard
¼ teaspoon tabasco sauce, if desired

Simply mix the ingredients.

Chicken 'n' Stuffing Scallop

3½ cups herb-seasoned stuffing
3 cups cubed cooked or canned chicken
½ cup butter or margarine
½ cup flour
¼ teaspoon salt
Dash of pepper
4 cups chicken broth
6 eggs, slightly beaten

Prepare stuffing according to package directions for dry stuffing. Spread in a 13x9x2-inch baking dish and top with chicken.

In a large saucepan, melt butter; blend in flour and seasonings. Add cool broth; cook and stir until mixture thickens. Stir small amount of hot mixture into eggs, return to hot mixture, pour over chicken. Bake in 325° oven for 40 to 45 minutes, or until knife inserted halfway to center comes out clean. Let stand 5 minutes to set; cut in squares and serve with pimiento-mushroom sauce.

Pimiento-Mushroom Sauce

1 can condensed cream of mushroom soup
1 cup dairy sour cream
¼ cup milk
¼ cup chopped pimiento

Combine ingredients; heat, stirring, until hot. Do not let mixture boil.

Pork Chop Dinner

4 to 8 pork chops	2 or 3 onions
Salt, pepper, and flour mixture	1 can beef broth or vegetable soup
3 or 4 large potatoes	1 can water

Roll pork chops in the flour mixture; fry until brown. In a baking dish put a layer of potatoes, a layer of onions, salt and pepper. Place the chops on top and pour on the beef broth or vegetable soup, and water. Cover and bake at 375° about 50 minutes. Uncover and brown.

Sausage Skillet

1 pound pork sausage meat	2 cups tomatoes
1/4 cup chopped onion	1/2 cup chili sauce
3 cups cooked rice	

Cook rice according to package directions. In skillet, fry crumbled sausage meat and onion until lightly browned. Stir with spatula to fry uniformly. Drain off fat. Add cooked rice, tomatoes, and chili sauce. Blend thoroughly. Cover. Cook over a low flame for 30 minutes. Serves 6.

Chicken Corn Soup

1 4- or 5-pound chicken	Parsley sprigs
Salt and pepper	3 cups corn

Put chicken in pot and cook slowly until all meat leaves the bones. Take out and remove meat from bones. Put back into stock and season well with salt and pepper to taste. Add small sprigs of parsley, three cups of fresh or canned corn; simmer till thoroughly heated and corn is done. Serve in soup bowls with homemade bread or crackers.

This 'n' That

Cheese Balls

1 heaping tablespoon salad dressing
8-ounce package cream cheese
Grated cheese
1 wedge bleu cheese
½ cup finely cut celery
Crushed nuts

Soften bleu cheese and blend with cream cheese and salad dressing. Add celery and some crushed nuts. Shape cheese mix into balls, allowing about 1 teaspoonful to each ball. Coat balls with grated cheese. Chill. Serve on toothpicks.

Party Mix

6 tablespoons butter or margarine
4 teaspoons Worcestershire sauce
1 teaspoon seasoned salt or ⅜ teaspoon garlic powder and ⅜ teaspoon salt
6 cups mixed dry cereal (mix wheat, corn, and rice cereals)
¾ cup salted nuts

Heat oven to 250°. Slowly melt butter in shallow pan. Stir in Worcestershire sauce and salt or substitute. Add cereal and nuts. Mix until all pieces are coated. Heat in oven 45 minutes. Stir every 15 minutes. Spread on absorbent paper to cool. Yield 6¾ cups.

▲ ▲ ▲

There is not a tissue in the human body that is removed from the influence of the spirit.
—*British Medical Journal*

▼ ▼ ▼

Chipped Beef and Cream Cheese Dip

1 jar chipped beef
2 packages cream cheese (3 ounces each)
½ cup cream
Onion juice to taste

Sauté beef in a little butter or margarine until crisp. Cool, then crumble. Cream the cheese well; add cream and blend. Season to taste with the onion juice; stir in sauteed beef. Serve with potato chips.

Eggs Goldenrod

6 hard-boiled eggs
2 cups medium white sauce
6 slices buttered hot toast

Cut hard-cooked eggs in halves lengthwise; cut egg whites in long slices and add to sauce. Serve on slices of hot toast. Force egg yolks through sieve and scatter over top of bread.

Raisin Sauce

1 cup raisins
2 cups water
. . .
2 tablespoons cornstarch
2 tablespoons sugar
⅛ teaspoon salt
2 tablespoons cold water
1 tablespoon butter
2 tablespoons lemon juice, if desired
1 tablespoon vinegar, if desired

Simmer raisins in water for 15 minutes. Combine cornstarch, sugar, salt, and 2 tablespoons cold water to make a paste. Add to raisins and heat until thickened. Remove from heat. Add butter and/or lemon juice and/or vinegar.

▲ ▲ ▲

Love, which is the essence of God, is not for levity, but for the total worth of man.
—*Ralph Waldo Emerson*

▼ ▼ ▼

Jellied Cranberry Sauce

1 pound cranberries (4 cups)	2 cups sugar
	2 cups water

Wash cranberries; place them, sugar, and water in deep saucepan and bring to a boil; cover and cook slowly for 20 minutes. If covered too tightly at first, there is a tendency for them to boil over. Approximate yield: 4 cups.

Baked Beans

2 pounds soup beans	1 tablespoon dry mustard
2 pound-cans tomatoes	½ pound sliced bacon
½ cup molasses	1 bottle of catsup

Soak beans in water for 12 hours. Drain. Cover with salted water, simmer slowly 1 to 1½ hours. Drain. Put in greased baking dish. Mix ingredients together, except bacon, and add to beans. Lay slices of bacon on top of beans. Bake in moderate oven (350°) about 30 minutes or until bacon gets a little brown.

Boiled Salad Dressing

2 tablespoons butter	2 teaspoons sugar
1 tablespoon flour	1 teaspoon dry mustard
2 eggs	⅔ teaspoon salt
1 cup vinegar	⅓ teaspoon pepper

Put butter, flour, sugar, eggs, mustard, salt, and pepper into a bowl or the top part of a double boiler and cook over hot water till they begin to thicken. Add vinegar and continue cooking three minutes. Beat mixture occasionally while cooling. Keep in a cool dark place. This dressing will remain good several weeks.

Raspberry Jam

- 3 10-ounce packages frozen red raspberries
- 5 cups sugar
- 1 box fruit pectin
- 1 cup water

Crush thawed raspberries and measure 3½ cups thawed fruit into large pan. Measure sugar and set aside. Mix fruit pectin and water in small saucepan. Bring to full rolling boil and boil for 1 minute, stirring constantly. Add to the fruit and then add sugar and stir for one minute. Ladle into glasses or freezer containers. Cover at once with tight lids or seals. Let stand 24 hours. Store in freezer, or if jam is to be used within 2 weeks, store in refrigerator.

Chili Sauce

- 1 10-pound basket tomatoes
- 1 quart onions
- 3 red sweet peppers
- 3 green peppers
- ½ cup salt
- 3 pounds brown sugar
- 1 pint cider vinegar
- ¼ ounce ground cloves
- 1 ounce white mustard seed
- ½ ounce celery seed
- 1 teaspoon black pepper
- Salt to taste
- 1 teaspoon red pepper, optional

Grind tomatoes, onions, and peppers together. Add remaining ingredients. Boil slowly until thick, stirring so it will not burn. Ladle into jars when cool and seal.

▲ ▲ ▲

"It is not necessary to hope in order to undertake, nor to succeed in order to persevere."
—*William the Silent*

▼ ▼ ▼

Grape Jelly

3 cups sugar   6 cups grapes, washed

Heat grapes until juice flows freely. Strain through cheesecloth in a colander. Cook juice until it comes to a rolling boil; then add 3 cups sugar and stir until dissolved. Boil very briefly. Pour into jelly glasses. It thickens as it cools.

Cranberry-Orange Relish

All-sugar recipe
4 cups cranberries
2 oranges
2 cups sugar

No-sugar recipe
4 cups cranberries
2 oranges
1 cup marmalade or jelly
1 cup corn syrup

Put cranberries through food chopper. Quarter whole oranges, but do not peel. Remove seeds and put fruit through chopper. Add marmalade and corn syrup (or sugar) and mix well. Chill a few hours before serving. Makes 1 quart.

Strawberry Preserves

1 quart stemmed washed strawberries
4 cups sugar
2 tablespoons lemon juice

Mix one quart strawberries, after they are stemmed and washed, and 2 cups sugar. Let boil 5 minutes. Then add 2 more cups sugar and 2 tablespoons lemon juice. Cook 15 minutes. Stir just enough to keep from boiling over. Let set overnight or until it gets cold. Put in sterilized jars with paraffin wax on top. If I make more than one box, I make a box at a time, and pour all together in an enamel pot or dishpan to cool.

Pastries and Pies

Raisin Custard Pie

⅔ cup sugar
1½ cups raisins
2 tablespoons cornstarch
½ teaspoon salt
½ teaspoon cloves
2 eggs, well beaten
1½ cups milk
⅓ cup water

Rinse and drain raisins. Spread in unbaked pie shell. Mix together the sugar, cornstarch, salt, and cloves. Add mixture to well-beaten eggs. Stir into milk and water. Pour this custard mixture carefully over raisins in pie shell. Bake at 375° for 50 or 60 minutes.

Peach Custard Pie

Prepare a baked pie shell at least 2 inches deep. Cool and fill ⅔ full with sliced, sugared peaches. Cover the peaches at once with a layer of cold cooked custard and spread the custard with a layer of whipped cream, slightly sweetened. Chill before serving.

Custard: Scald 2 cups milk. Beat 3 eggs and add ½ cup sugar mixed with 3 tablespoons cornstarch and ¼ teaspoon salt. Stir the hot milk gradually into egg mixture in the saucepan, and stir over a slow heat until thickened. Cool slightly; add ¼ teaspoon almond extract and pour over peaches when cold.

▲ ▲ ▲

"Goodness is the only investment that never fails."

—*Ralph Waldo Emerson*

▼ ▼ ▼

Peach Cobbler

¼ cup soft oleo	2 teaspoons baking powder
½ cup sugar	¼ teaspoon salt
. . .	½ cup milk
1 cup flour	1 can sliced peaches

Cream oleo and sugar. Sift together flour, baking powder, and salt. Stir into shortening alternately with ½ cup milk. Beat until smooth. Pour into 8-inch square pan. Put over the batter sliced peaches. Lay slices close together. Pour about ¼ cup of the peach juice over the peaches and batter. Bake 45 minutes in about 350° oven.

Serve with milk or ice cream.

Applesauce Custard Pie

1 medium can applesauce	⅔ cup sugar
2 eggs	1 cup evaporated milk
3 tablespoons melted butter	2 teaspoons cinnamon

Beat eggs in applesauce; add sugar and mix. Stir in canned milk and melted butter. Pour in a 9-inch unbaked crust; sprinkle on cinnamon. Bake 350° until filling is firm.

Apple Streusel Pie

Streusel topping: Make a pastry for a two-crust pie, mixing the shortening into the flour. Take out one cup of this mixture and add to it ⅓ cup brown sugar and ½ teaspoon cinnamon. Mix this and keep it for the streusel topping.

Pare and slice 7 or 8 apples; add 1 cup sugar and 1 teaspoon cinnamon. Mix well. Fill pastry-lined pan with apples. Dot with butter. Sprinkle the streusel topping on the apples. Bake 50 to 60 minutes in hot oven at 425°.

Bohemian Pastries

½ pound butter or margarine
½ pound cream cheese
1 teaspoon lemon juice
2 cups sifted flour
2 tablespoons sugar
Apricot or raspberry preserves

Cream butter or margarine and cheese. Blend in lemon juice and add sifted dry ingredients. Chill in refrigerator several hours. Roll very thin and cut into small squares. Dot with fruit filling. Press 2 opposite corners of dough together to seal in filling. Bake at 450° for 10 to 15 minutes.

Shoo Fly Pie

1½ cups flour
1 teaspoon baking powder
. . .
½ cup dark molasses
1 teaspoon soda
¾ cup boiling water
½ cup sugar (brown and white mixed)
4 tablespoons shortening
Unbaked pie crust

Combine into a crumb mixture the flour, baking powder, sugar, and shortening. Combine molasses, soda, and boiling water. Pour ⅓ liquid into pastry-lined pie pan. Sprinkle ⅓ of crumbs over liquid. Continue alternating, ending with crumbs. Bake at 350° for 30 minutes.

▲ ▲ ▲

"Age does not depend upon years, but upon temperament and health. Some men are born old and some never grow old."
—*Tryon Edwards*

▼ ▼ ▼

Lemon Chiffon Pie

1 envelope unflavored gelatin
¼ cup cold water
4 eggs
1 cup sugar
½ cup lemon juice
½ teaspoon salt
1 teaspoon grated lemon rind
Baked pie shell

Add ½ cup sugar, lemon juice, and salt to beaten egg yolks and cook over boiling water until custard consistency. Pour cold water in bowl and sprinkle gelatin on top of water. Add to hot custard and stir until dissolved. Add grated lemon rind. Cool. When mixture begins to thicken, fold in stiffly beaten egg whites to which other ½ cup of sugar has been added. Fill baked pie shell or graham cracker crust and chill. Just before serving, if you wish, spread over pie a thin layer of whipped cream.

Satin Pie

12-ounce chocolate bits
¼ cup milk
¼ cup sugar
4 eggs, separated
Pinch of salt
Whipped cream
Baked pie shell

Melt chocolate bits, milk, sugar, and salt over hot water. Cool; beat in egg yolks one at a time. Beat egg whites until stiff, fold in chocolate mixture and pour into baked crust. Top with whipped cream when ready to serve; a tablespoon of sugar and a few finely chopped nuts added to crust is good!

▲ ▲ ▲

"Beware of despairing of yourself; you are commanded to put your trust in God, not in yourself."

—*Augustine*

▼ ▼ ▼

French Cream Cherry Pie

No. 2 can sour red cherries
2/3 cup sugar
3 tablespoons cornstarch
Pinch of salt
. . .
2 tablespoons butter
1/2 teaspoon almond flavoring
Pie shell material
1/2 pint whipped cream
Vanilla pudding

Drain juice from the can of sour red cherries. Mix the sugar, cornstarch, and salt. Add cherry juice and stir until sugar is dissolved. Cook over low heat, stirring constantly. When thickened, add cherries, butter, and almond flavoring. Cool, then pour over a pie shell filled with vanilla pudding. Top with whipped cream.

Fruit Cobbler

1 cup sugar
2 teaspoons baking powder
2 tablespoons butter (very soft)
1 cup flour
1 cup milk
Drained fruit

Beat everything together. Line baking dish with butter. Put layer of drained fruit in bottom of pan then layer of batter. Repeat layers. Bake 30 minutes at 350° or 375°. Suggestions of fruit: fruit cocktail, peaches, pineapple, apricot, or any other sweetened fruit.

▲ ▲ ▲

Tomorrow is the longest day in the week, It has to be, because of the things we are going to do then.

▼ ▼ ▼

Lemon Sponge Pie

3 tablespoons shortening
⅛ teaspoon salt
¾ cup sugar
2½ tablespoons flour
2 egg whites, stiffly beaten
2 egg yolks
1 cup milk
Juice and grated rind of 1 lemon

Combine shortening, salt, sugar, and flour. Mix well. Add egg yolks, milk, lemon juice, and rind. Beat with rotary beater until smooth. Fold in beaten egg whites. Pour in unbaked pie shell. Bake in moderate oven about 40 minutes, or until brown.

Pecan Pie

1 cup pecans
3 eggs
½ cup sugar
1 cup dark corn syrup
⅛ teaspoon salt
¼ cup melted butter
1 teaspoon vanilla

Combine butter and sugar. Add syrup, eggs, salt, and vanilla. Mix thoroughly and add coarsely broken nutmeats. Pour into unbaked pie shell. Bake at 425° for ten minutes, then at 400° about 40 minutes longer until custard is firm. Cool before serving.

▲ ▲ ▲

May the colors and the blossoms bold
Warm your friends from the wind so cold.
—Author unknown

▼ ▼ ▼

Banana Split Pie

½ cup margarine
1½ cups powdered sugar
2 eggs
1 teaspoon vanilla
1 square grated baking chocolate

. . .
1 tablespoon lemon juice
2 bananas, sliced
¼ cup nuts
Pie shell

Beat together margarine and sifted, powdered sugar. Add eggs, 1 at a time, beating 3 minutes after each. Add vanilla. Add 1 square grated baking chocolate. Mix lemon juice with 2 bananas, sliced. Reserve about 12 banana slices to decorate top. Fold in sliced bananas, filling cooled baked pie shell. Nuts may be put on top. Refrigerate two hours (no baking).

Strawberry Glace Pie

Baked pie shell
1 quart strawberries
1 cup water
1 cup sugar

3 tablespoons cornstarch
1 3-ounce package cream cheese

Wash and hull strawberries. Cook 1 cup strawberries and ⅔ cup water 4 minutes. Blend cornstarch, sugar, and ⅓ cup water and add to boiling mixture. Stir constantly and boil about 1 minute. Cool mixture. Spread softened cream cheese on bottom of pie shell. Put uncooked berries in pie shell and cover with cooled, cooked mixture. Refrigerate and serve with whipped cream.

▲ ▲ ▲

A mouse perched jauntily on an elephant's back crossed a rickety bridge. The mouse said, "Didn't WE make that bridge shake?"

▼ ▼ ▼

Christmas Pie

Crust: Mix 1½ cups finely ground nutmeats with 3 tablespoons sugar. Press into 9-inch pie plate and bake for 8 minutes in 400° oven.

Filling: Soak 1 envelope unflavored gelatin in ¼ cup water. Cook 3 egg yolks, beaten, ¼ cup sugar, ⅛ teaspoon salt, and 1½ cups scalded milk in double boiler until it coats a metal spoon. Stir in gelatin. Cool and chill. Beat with egg beater and add ½ cup maraschino cherries. Beat 3 egg whites and add ¼ cup sugar. Add to first mixture. Pour into baked pie shell and chill.

French Mint Pie

- 9-inch baked graham cracker crust
- ¼ pound butter or margarine
- 1 cup confectioners' sugar
- 2 eggs
- 2 2-ounce squares unsweetened chocolate
- ½ teaspoon peppermint flavoring or 2 drops peppermint oil

Cream together butter, confectioners' sugar, and eggs until very smooth. Melt chocolate over hot water (do not scorch) and cool; stir into above mixture. Stir in flavoring (be careful if using the peppermint oil—this is very concentrated). Pour filling into baked crust. Chill at least 12 hours. Serve topped with whipped cream.

▲ ▲ ▲

"Life is not so short but that there is always time enough for courtesy."

—Emerson

▼ ▼ ▼

Autumn Gold Pumpkin Pie

- 3 large eggs
- ½ cup sugar
- 1 cup melted butter or ½ cup of cream
- 1 cup mashed cooked pumpkin
- ¾ cup dark corn syrup
- ½ cup coarsely chopped nuts
- ¼ teaspoon salt
- 1 teaspoon cinnamon
- ½ teaspoon ginger
- ½ teaspoon nutmeg

Mix ingredients (except nuts) and beat thoroughly. Add nuts. Bake 45 to 50 minutes in quick oven—375°. If nuts are not used in the filling, top may be garnished with nuts. Serve topped with whipped cream.

Butterscotch Pie

- 1½ cups brown sugar
- 1½ cups water
- 3 tablespoons flour
- 3 tablespoons cornstarch
- 2 tablespoons white sugar
- 2 egg yolks
- 3 tablespoons butter
- ⅛ teaspoon salt
- 1 teaspoon vanilla

Heat brown sugar and water to boiling point and pour over sifted flour, cornstarch, and white sugar. Cook until thick. Add slightly beaten egg yolks. Cook one minute longer. Remove from fire. Add butter, salt, and vanilla. Let cool, and pour into pie shell.

▲ ▲ ▲

"Cheerfulness and content are great beautifiers and are famous preservers of youthful looks."

—*Charles Dickens*

▼ ▼ ▼

Custard Pie

Plain pastry for one 9-inch pie:
1 cup sifted flour
⅓ cup shortening
1 teaspoon salt
4 to 5 tablespoons cold water

Cut shortening into salt and flour mixture. Sprinkle water, tablespoon at a time, over mixture. Mix with fork; pour onto waxed paper and form into ball. Let stand a few minutes. Flatten slightly and roll on lightly floured pastry cloth. Roll dough and fit 9-inch shell.

Filling:
4 slightly beaten eggs
½ cup sugar
¼ teaspoon salt
½ teaspoon vanilla
½ teaspoon almond extract
2½ cups scalded milk
Nutmeg

Blend eggs, sugar, salt, vanilla, and almond extract. Gradually stir in scalded milk. Pour into chilled unbaked pie shell. Bake at 400° for 25 to 30 minutes. Remove from oven and sprinkle with nutmeg.

Cream Pie

⅓ cup flour
⅔ cup sugar
¼ teaspoon salt
2 cups milk, scalded
3 slightly beaten egg yolks
½ teaspoon vanilla
1 9-inch baked shell
3 stiffly beaten egg whites
6 tablespoons sugar
2 tablespoons butter or margarine

Mix flour, ⅔ cup sugar, and salt; gradually add heated milk. Cook in double boiler until thick, stirring often. Add small amount to egg yolks; then pour back into remaining hot mixture and cook 2 minutes longer. Cool. Add butter and vanilla. Pour into baked shell and cover with meringue made of egg whites and 6 tablespoons sugar. Bake in moderate oven 350° about 12 minutes.

Salads

Frozen Fruit Salad

⅓ cup chopped nuts
3 tablespoons chopped maraschino cherries, drained well
1 9-ounce can crushed pineapple, drained
1 pint sour cream
¾ cup sugar
2 tablespoons lemon juice
⅓ teaspoon salt
1 banana, diced

Combine ingredients and stir together gently but well. Spoon into one dozen paper muffin pan liners. Freeze. Remove paper before serving.

Raggedy Ann Salad

Half a hard-boiled egg, cut lengthwise
1 tablespoon shredded carrot
Half of small tomato
2 small sweet pickles (Gherkins)
2 lettuce leaves
1 portion crabmeat or tuna fish salad (consisting of fish, chopped celery and mayonnaise)
Cloves for eyes and nose
Narrow strip of pimiento for mouth

Place egg at top (yolk-side down); arrange shredded carrot around egg to represent hair; make face on egg with cloves and pimiento. Below egg, place half tomato, round side up, for body; place pickles horizontally at each side of tomato (arms); at bottom of tomato, place fish salad; over salad, arrange lettuce leaves to resemble skirt. Recipe makes an individual serving.

▲ ▲ ▲

I am a part of all that I have met.
—Alfred Tennyson

▼ ▼ ▼

Apricot-Pineapple Salad

2 boxes orange gelatin
2 cups hot water
1 cup combined fruit juice
. . .
1 large can apricots, cut in small pieces
1 medium can crushed pineapple
1 cup miniature marshmallows
½ cup sugar
3 tablespoons flour
1 cup combined fruit juices
1 egg, beaten
½ pint whipped cream
Grated cheese

Mix gelatin, hot water, and fruit juice. Chill liquid. Add apricots, pineapple, and marshmallows. Chill until set. Combine sugar, flour, fruit juices, and beaten egg. Cook until thick. Cool. Fold 1 cup of whipped cream into this mixture. Spread over jello and sprinkle grated cheese on top.

Potato Salad

6 diced potatoes (well-cooked and still warm)
1 medium-sized onion, diced fine
1 cup diced Pascal celery
1 cup diced sweet pickles
¼ cup vinegar
¼ cup sweet pickle juice
1 cup mayonnaise
2 tablespoons prepared hot horseradish
3 tablespoons sugar
Dash of pepper
Dash of salt

Blend ingredients in the order given. Blending and mixing well while potatoes are still warm makes this salad creamy. Sprinkle lightly with paprika and center with sprig of celery.

Six-Cup Salad

1 cup sour cream
1 cup nuts
1 cup coconut
1 cup marshmallows
1 cup mandarin oranges
1 cup pineapple chunks

Mix ingredients together lightly. Can be served immediately or keeps well if made ahead of time. Serve with crackers.

Orange Sherbet Salad

- 2 3-ounce packages orange gelatin
- 2 cups boiling water
- 2 cans mandarin oranges drained and cut in half
- ¾ cup juice from oranges
- 1 pint orange sherbet

Dissolve gelatin in hot water; add juice from oranges and stir in orange sherbet. When mixture begins to set, add mandarin oranges. Chill until firm; 10 servings.

Cranberry Waldorf Salad

- 1 can jellied or whole cranberry sauce
- 1 envelope plain gelatin
- ½ cup cold water
- ½ cup diced celery
- ½ cup diced apples
- 2 tablespoons chopped nutmeats

Heat cranberry sauce to boiling. Soften gelatin in cold water for 5 minutes. Add to cranberry sauce and stir until thoroughly dissolved. Cool. Add celery, apples and nuts. Pour into molds and chill until firm.

Pineapple-Cheese Salad

- 1 package lemon gelatin
- 1 cup hot water
- 1 cup pineapple juice
- 1 cup crushed pineapple
- ¼ cup maraschino cherries
- 1 8-ounce package of cream cheese

Dissolve gelatin in hot water. Add pineapple juice and chill. Mix with cheese 2 tablespoons cherry juice or cream. When smooth, combine cheese with crushed pineapple and chopped cherries. When gelatin begins to thicken, add salad mixture. Pour into mold and chill until firm. Unmold on lettuce and garnish with mayonnaise and olives. Serves 4 to 6.

German Potato Salad

¼ cup light vinegar	1 small onion
2 tablespoons sugar	3 tablespoons water
Pepper to taste	1 teaspoon salt
Few celery leaves, chopped fine	Small amount of celery seed

. . .

¼ pound bacon	Potatoes

Cook potatoes and cut in any style you like. Fry slightly the bacon and onion. Mix ingredients together and pour over potatoes and mix. A sweet red or green pepper may be sliced fine to add color and flavor. If a large amount is needed, the seasonings should be doubled or tripled, according to the amount of potatoes used.

Cranberry Fluff

2 cups raw cranberries, ground	½ cup seedless green grapes
3 cups miniature marshmallows	⅓ cup broken walnuts
¾ cup sugar	¼ teaspoon salt
. . .	1 cup heavy cream, whipped
2 cups diced unpared apples	Lettuce

Combine cranberries, marshmallows, and sugar. Cover and chill overnight. Add apples, grapes, walnuts, and salt. Fold in whipped cream. Chill. Spoon into individual lettuce cups. Makes 8 to 10 servings.

▲ ▲ ▲

Fear not that thy life shall come to an end, but rather fear that it shall never have a beginning.

—*J. H. Newman*

▼ ▼ ▼

Baked Chicken Salad

- 2 cups cooked chopped chicken
- 2 cups cooked fluffy rice
- 1 cup chopped celery
- ½ cup slivered almonds or chopped pecans
- 3 tablespoons grated onion
- 2 tablespoons fresh lemon juice
- 3 hard-boiled eggs, diced
- ½ cup salad dressing
- 1 can cream of chicken soup
- Salt and pepper

Mix all together carefully; and if mixture is too dry or stiff, add ½ cup broth.

Place in flat dish and cover with crushed potato chips. Bake uncovered in 350° oven for 30 minutes. Will serve 6 to 8 as a main dish. Can be made sometime before serving.

Tomorrow's Salad

- 2 eggs
- ¼ cup sugar
- ¼ cup vinegar
- 2 tablespoons butter
- . . .
- 2 cups miniature marshmallows
- 2 cups diced pineapple
- ¼ cup maraschino cherries
- 2 cups white cherries
- 1 orange, diced
- 1 cup heavy cream, whipped

Beat eggs; add sugar and vinegar. Cook over low heat until thick and smooth. Remove from heat and stir in butter. Pit cherries; dice pineapple, cherries, and orange and mix together with vinegar dressing. Fold in whipped cream and let stand in refrigerator 24 hours.

▲ ▲ ▲

"My business is not to remake myself, but to make the absolute best of what God made."
—*Robert Browning*

▼ ▼ ▼

Coke and Bing Cherry Salad

1 large can crushed pineapple
1 large can Bing cherries
1 cup pecans
2 small bottles Coca-Cola (12 oz. total)
1 8-ounce package cream cheese
2 packages cherry gelatin

Drain fruit. Heat juice from fruit and enough water to make 2 cups liquid. Dissolve gelatin. Cool. Add chopped cherries, nuts, cream cheese, cold Cokes and pineapple. Chill until set. Serves 16.

Twenty-Four-Hour Bean Salad

1 15½-ounce can cut wax beans
1 16-ounce can French-style green beans
1 17-ounce can kidney beans
1 cup thinly sliced onions
½ cup cider vinegar
½ cup granulated sugar
½ teaspoon salt
¼ teaspoon pepper
½ cup salad oil

Day before serving, combine all beans, drained, with onions. Combine oil, vinegar, sugar, salt, and pepper in jar; shake well until blended. Pour over beans; cover and refrigerate until served, tossing occasionally.

To serve, drain dressing from bean mixture and pile beans lightly on lettuce or chicory on salad dish. Serves 12.

▲ ▲ ▲

"In the midst of winter I suddenly found that there was in me an invincible summer."
—*Albert Camus*

▼ ▼ ▼

Pineapple Harlequin

1 package lime-flavored gelatin	1 package lemon-flavored gelatin
1½ cups boiling water	1½ cups boiling water
2 tablespoons fresh, frozen, or canned lemon juice	2 tablespoons fresh, frozen or canned lemon juice
1 cup drained, crushed pineapple	. . .
1 3-ounce package cream cheese	Lettuce
	Salad dressing

Prepare lime-flavored gelatin accordiing to directions on package, using 1½ cups boiling water; add 2 tablespoons lemon juice. Chill until slightly thickened. Add crushed pineapple. If desired, garnish mold with diced pineapple.

Pour half of lime-pineapple mixture into 1-pound coffee can. Chill until firm.

Dissolve lemon-flavored gelatin according to directions on package, using 1½ cups boiling water; add 2 tablespoons lemon juice. Chill until slightly thickened. Whip until light and fluffy. Beat in cream cheese. Pour over lime-pineapple mixture. Chill until firm. Pour remaining slightly thickened lime-pineapple mixture over lemon-cheese layer. Chill until firm. Unmold on serving platter. Garnish with lettuce and serve with salad dressing.

Seafoods

Crab Festival

- 1½ cups flaked, fresh crab meat
- 1 tablespoon butter
- 1 tablespoon bread crumbs
- ¾ cup cream
- 2 eggs
- ¼ teaspoon pepper
- 1 tablespoon mustard
- 3 tablespoons melted butter
- 1 teaspoon paprika

In saucepan, melt butter. Add bread crumbs and cream. Cook until thick; stir constantly. Remove from flame. Beat eggs; add eggs and seasonings. Add crab meat. Mix thoroughly. Pack into crab shells or individual casseroles. Brush each crab with melted butter and sprinkle with paprika. Brown in a hot oven (400°) for 10 minutes.

Scalloped Oysters

- 1 pint oysters
- 3 cups coarse cracker crumbs
- ¾ teaspoon salt
- Few grains pepper
- 2 tablespoons parsley
- ¾ cup milk
- ½ cup oyster liquid
- ⅓ cup melted butter

Remove shell from oysters, and drain. Place a layer of crackers in greased casserole; add layer of oysters, salt, pepper, parsley, ending with crackers. Combine milk, oyster liquid, and butter. Pour from side of dish. Bake 30 minutes at 350°.

▲ ▲ ▲

Still as of old
Men by themselves are priced—
For thirty pieces Judas sold
Himself, not Christ.
  —Hester H. Cholmondeley

▼ ▼ ▼

Tuna and Noodle Casserole

2 cups cooked noodles
1 7-ounce can tuna
1 16-ounce can cream of mushroom soup
¼ cup water
Bread crumbs

Cook and drain 2 cups noodles. Combine noodles, 1 7-ounce can tuna, 1 16-ounce can condensed cream of mushroom soup, and ¼ cup water. Place in greased ovenproof dish, top with bread crumbs and bake in 450° oven until top is brown.

Seafood Fancy

¾ cup chopped green pepper
¾ cup chopped onion
1 cup diced celery
1 cup crab meat
1 cup diced shrimp
½ teaspoon salt
Dash pepper
1 teaspoon Worcestershire sauce
1 cup mayonnaise
. . .
1 cup bread crumbs
2 tablespoons melted butter

Combine vegetables, crab meat, shrimp, salt, pepper, Worcestershire sauce, and mayonnaise. Place in greased 1-quart casserole or 6 baking shells. Toss crumbs in butter and sprinkle over the top. Bake at 360° for 30 minutes or until hot and crumbs are brown.

▲ ▲ ▲

Nothing before, nothing behind;
The steps of faith
Fall on the seeming void, and find
The rock beneath.
        —*John Greenleaf Whittier*

▼ ▼ ▼

Shrimp Delight

1 dozen shrimp	Parmesan cheese
1/3 cup crab meat, shredded	Concentrated garlic
	Butter
3/4 cup cracker crumbs	Lemon or lime slices

Cook shrimp and break into small pieces—about three or four pieces per shrimp. Mix in crab meat. Place in individual baking shells or casseroles, cover with cracker crumbs. Sprinkle with cheese and saturate with concentrated garlic. Top with a dab of butter. Place under broiler to brown. Garnish with lemon or lime slice. Makes four servings.

Crab Appetizers

1 tablespoon chopped onion	1 cup crab meat
1 tablespoon melted shortening	1/2 teaspoon Worcestershire sauce
2 1/2 tablespoons flour	Salt and pepper
1/2 cup cream	1/2 cup dry bread crumbs

Cook onion in shortening until tender. Stir in flour; gradually add cream and cook, stirring constantly until the mixture thickens. Carefully remove all shell particles from crab meat and add meat to the white sauce along with the Worcestershire sauce. Salt and pepper to taste. Mix well and cool. When cool enough to handle, drop the mixture by teaspoonfuls into the bread crumbs and roll into small balls. Place in greased pan and broil, turning to brown all sides, or, if preferred, fry in deep fat (390°) about 2 minutes or until brown. Serve either hot or cold on toothpicks. Makes 3 1/2 dozen.

Vegetables

Scalloped Asparagus

2 cans asparagus spears
1½ cups seasoned
   white sauce
Ritz crackers
Butter

Mix asparagus and white sauce. Cover with buttered Ritz cracker crumbs. Bake at 325° until golden brown and bubbly.

Green Bean Casserole

2 cans green beans
1 can cream of
   mushroom soup
3 tablespoons milk
Grated cheese or French
   fried onion rings

Dilute soup with milk. Mix drained green beans with soup. Top with cheese or onion rings and bake at 350° about 30 minutes.

Scalloped Cabbage

5 cups shredded raw
   cabbage
2 cups medium white sauce
1 cup grated cheese
2 tablespoons fine crumbs

Mix cabbage and white sauce in 1½-quart baking dish. Top with grated cheese and crumbs. Bake in moderately hot oven 400° about 20 minutes, until tender. Serves 6.

▲ ▲ ▲

*Though my soul may set in darkness, it will rise
   in perfect light,
I have loved the stars too fondly to be fearful
   of the night.*

—Sarah Williams

▼ ▼ ▼

Carrots

Slice carrots diagonally. Add a little bit of water and a dash of salt. Cover tightly and cook slowly so they won't burn. During last 10 minutes lay 3 cloves of garlic on top. When tender, remove garlic and serve!

Corn Fritters

1 cup flour	1 egg
1½ teaspoons baking powder	¼ cup milk
1 tablespoon sugar	½ cup canned whole kernel corn
1 teaspoon salt, scant	Deep fat, for frying
Confectioners' sugar	

Sift flour, baking powder, sugar, and salt together. Add egg, milk, and corn. Stir until well blended. Drop batter into 350° fat by teaspoonfuls. Fry until golden brown, turning once to cook evenly. Drain fritters on paper. Place on serving platter and sprinkle with confectioners' sugar. Makes about 16 fritters.

Sweet Potato Balls

4 medium sweet potatoes, cooked and mashed	Crushed cereal flakes
3 tablespoons brown sugar, packed	Marshmallows

Drop sweet potato mixture onto waxed paper containing crushed cereal flakes. Before rolling into ball place a marshmallow in the center. Roll in cereal and fry in deep fat to a golden brown.

▲ ▲ ▲

I am not bound to win,
But I am bound to be true.
—*Abraham Lincoln*

▼ ▼ ▼

Harvard Beets

3 cups sliced or diced beets
½ cup water
½ cup sugar
2 tablespoons flour
½ teaspoon salt
2 tablespoons butter
¼ cup vinegar

Mix flour, sugar, and salt together. Add vinegar and water. Cook until thick. Add butter. Add cooked beets and reheat. Serves 6.

Corn Pudding

2 cups cream-style corn
2 eggs, well beaten
1 teaspoon sugar
1 teaspoon salt
¼ teaspoon pepper
1 tablespoon butter
4 tablespoons cracker crumbs

Heat oven to 350°. Mix ingredients except cracker crumbs and pour into baking dish. Cover with crumbs and bake for 1 hour.

▲ ▲ ▲

Prayer means opening every channel of our lives to the "deep health" and "quiet glory" of God.

▼ ▼ ▼